ALIGN THE BOARD AND CEO

ALIGN THE BOARD AND CEO

8 Steps for Nonprofit Leaders to Overcome
Dysfunction and Achieve Synergy

Michael D. Ward

ISBN: 979-8-89316-552-4 (Paperback)
ISBN: 979-8-89316-551-7 (Ebook)
ISBN: 979-8-89316-507-4 (Hardcover)

The framework you will read about in the book brings together all other elements into a board calendar that ensures the Board and CEO are truly aligned as you move through the year.

Please share your email so I can keep in touch with you, and I'll send you a Board Calendar Tool that you can use to deploy your learning. Follow this link to do so:

https://yourcfoadviser.com/align-welcome

DEDICATION

I dedicate this book to all of the people with whom I have worked in the nonprofit sector over the years, as well as the people we served.

The insights I share in this book came from my work with hundreds of fellow board members, nonprofit leaders, and colleagues in the sector.

I have remained engaged in the sector for over 25 years because of the people we serve, inspired by what they accomplish in their lives regardless of the challenges they may face. I am honored to have supported work that enables them to live their lives fully with dignity and purpose, and most importantly enjoy their rightful place as members of our community.

We are stronger for what we can learn from everyone around us.

CONTENTS

INTRODUCTION

After 25 years working within and for the nonprofit sector as an executive, board member, and consultant, I have developed the Nonprofit Board Synergy Framework, eight steps to align around best practices to drive ultimate organizational success. For those of you serving as a board member of a nonprofit organization or in a staff or management role, thank you for your contribution to this sector! Very important work is accomplished every day through the nonprofit sector, which, in many cases, is uniquely organized and structured to deliver.

For those of us fortunate to have worked in the nonprofit sector or served on the board, it can be one of the most rewarding experiences because we can see the impact of our efforts. If you are interested in joining the board or staff of a nonprofit organization for the first time, recently joined one, or have completed several years of service, you likely have questions about the role and how to better understand how you relate to others. The sector benefits from the broad range of experiences people bring to their roles, and this book will help them share a common language and understanding.

I've seen the greatest organizational success when boards, the chief executive and management teams are truly aligned, beyond just vision and mission. This book was written to give you a process and tools to achieve true alignment and take organizational performance to the next level. Some may wonder whether too much collaboration may undermine the objectivity of the board in holding the executive and management team accountable. As you'll see throughout the book, the board, chief executive, and management team have distinct roles in moving the organization forward and sustaining excellence. Having served in and consulted with each of those roles, I have seen organizations excel because each member of this collective worked well with the others without losing the ability to respectfully hold each other accountable. My learning has been affirmed most recently by my experience as a member of the board of Children's National Hospital, which has really gotten this right.

Alignment of nonprofit boards and management is critical because the sector has such a major impact on our society. The organization Independent Sector has supported the nonprofit sector for more than 40 years, during which the sector has grown substantially. Independent Sector reports that the nonprofit sector in 2023 contributed about 5.4% of the U.S. gross domestic product (GDP) and employs about 6.7% of the U.S. workforce.[1] IRS data on the nonprofit sector for 2024 shows it comprises at least 1.9 million entities that have applied for exemption who indicate they are active – and while churches and church affiliated organizations are not required to apply for exemption, some do and those who register would be included in that count. The sector not only responds to important needs in our communities, but at this scale also fuels

---

[1]   Health of the U.S. Nonprofit Sector, Annual Review, November 2023, published by Independent Sector.

them as employers and purchasers of other goods and services. It is therefore important that those leading organizations have the best tools and insights in raising and deploying resources in their work.

The economic pressures on the nonprofit sector today also make strong alignment an absolute priority. Many of you live this reality every day—it is hard to generate and sustain the resources to perform the work of the organization, to have them in hand when needed, and for them to be structured optimally for the work. Just over 2,700 foundations and just under 10,000 of all other exempt organizations have assets worth over $50,000,000, and about $5.5 trillion in aggregate. Less than 1% of the organizations hold about 58% of all the assets in the sector! Some of these may still have financial and liquidity challenges, but many with assets less than $50,000,000 must tightly manage their finances and cash flows.

How My Experience Informs this Approach

I first stepped into a boardroom over 25 years ago while serving as an accounting consultant for a mid-sized nonprofit organization. My role that day was to provide an update on my initial progress addressing some long-standing issues within the accounting function that prevented management from providing the board with timely financial information. I had just been brought in by another consultant who was serving as the interim Chief Financial Officer (CFO) to help him rebuild the accounting function. We spent several months working together to stabilize and update the accounting systems and processes. That consultant left after those few months, and I began working directly with the Chief Executive Officer (CEO) and moved into the CFO role.

I worked alongside the CEO for about three years, rebuilding the operations and the relationship with the board. At the three-year mark, the CEO stepped down, triggering a board search for a new CEO. As the search process began, one of the board members encouraged me to put my name in the hat, and I did so. During the search process, a long-tenured Vice President who was regarded as an expert in the field of our work served as the Interim CEO and I continued to serve in the CFO role. The search process spanned several months, during which I learned more about the complex corporate structure in which the organization functioned. I was ultimately appointed as the new CEO, a role in which I served for almost three years. It was one of the most rewarding phases in my career because I could see the impact of our work every day—our administrative offices were in the same building as our child development center, and I visited program sites throughout the year.

The organization was among three larger nonprofit organizations serving children and adults with intellectual and developmental disabilities based in the District of Columbia. These organizations worked both in the District and in the nearby counties in Maryland. The District government agencies that funded much of the work and were responsible for licensing and regulating the programs were under a consent decree and the oversight of a court monitor. While it was a challenging environment to operate in, I learned a lot about how governments structured funding for human services and how to navigate some of the politics and bureaucracy. I forged good working relationships with leaders of the government agencies funding our work and got more involved in the community of organizations doing similar work. I testified before the City Council a few times.

One of the most difficult decisions I had to make as CEO, requiring me to secure board support and approval to move forward, was to force a transition of several Medicaid funded facilities to another provider to save the rest of the organization. The programs had been operating at a sustained loss and the government refused to consider adjusting the rates—there was no mechanism to adjust funding as people aged and their needs changed. The only way to ensure enough funding was allocated—to support the individuals being served— was to have the government negotiate a new rate with a new provider. At a newly negotiated rate, they would pay another organization more, which would ensure enough resources to provide the support services to which the older residents were entitled. We designed the process so that the individuals we served, along with their families, would choose the new provider. I needed to ensure the board fully understood such complexities, as well as the financial and regulatory issues, and how we grounded the approach in the mission. Having a well-informed and aligned board was critical in getting to and executing the right decision here.

I also began serving on boards of other organizations while serving as CEO. At the time, I noticed differences in the relationship between management and the board of those organizations and the relationship I and my management team had with our board. Hearing discussions at the board level, I gained insight into board dynamics—some of which was that my fellow board members lacked the information they needed to govern effectively and make decisions. I saw how different management teams prepared for board meetings and board discussions, the types of issues they communicated, how they interacted with the boards, and the extent to which the boards and management were aligned to achieve the best outcomes for the organizations.

My work as CEO ended when my organization was merged into a larger, related organization. I transitioned back into the accounting profession in which I started my career, spending the next twenty years overseeing or providing outsourced accounting and CFO-level services to primarily nonprofit organizations. I also maintained my board roles and over time began serving on new boards. Moreover, I had the great honor to serve as board chair six times across several organizations and spanning more than a decade. As a board leader, I endeavored to learn as much as possible about the law, the role, and how to maximize my impact. Early on, I served for six years on the board of Mentors Inc. Other board roles spanned longer periods:

- For one system with multiple entities, my board service spanned over 20 years and included roles on the boards of a parent entity as well as two of the subsidiaries, serving as Chair, Vice Chair and Secretary at different points. I first served on the board of Health Services for Children with Special Needs, then moved to the HSC Foundation board, and for a period also served on the board of the HSC Pediatric Center. We collectively tackled significant and difficult investment decisions, organizational realignments, transitions in key leadership roles, and ultimately a merger.

- I also served on the board of National Children's Center (NCC), an organization similar to the one for which I served as CFO and CEO, spanning thirteen years, during which I served in several different roles, including as a trustee for the related foundation. NCC held a full-board membership in the National Association of Corporate Directors for four years during which we participated in numerous professional development opportunities and many of us attained the designation of Governance Fellow. During my service, we divested of an operating asset that generated a significant infusion into the foundation, completed an at-times challenging transformation of the board, made some significant program changes, and worked through several executive successions.

My contemporaneous board work served as a source of insight that I shared with clients to improve communications with their boards and build collaborative relationships, through which many of those organizations would thrive. As a consultant to nonprofit organizations, I have been frequently asked to provide training and guidance to boards and management on financial and accounting matters, so I realize how much of an information gap exists for those engaged in nonprofit work. As a nonprofit board member, I worked with the executives and management teams to refine and hone the information the board needed to most effectively support the work. I am now motivated to share what I learned from those experiences.

The Nonprofit Board Synergy Framework

The coming chapters in the book will provide you with an eight-step process to align on critical aspects of organizational functions, in which both management and the board have a role. My goal for you is to be able to have clear alignment among board, management and staff with role clarity and a shared understanding of the financial information about the organization, both in planning and subsequent financial reporting. Today's nonprofit organizations operate in a broad range of critical areas in our society, and their paths to raise and manage resources are more complicated than ever. The steps to align for success are as follows:

1. Confirm the legal structure
2. Clarify roles and responsibilities
3. Gain a shared understanding of the financial statements
4. Strengthen compliance and risk management practices
5. Develop a diversified resource generation strategy
6. Establish a robust planning and budgeting process
7. Implement resource management best practices
8. Map out an annual board calendar and follow it

You may well have some aspects of these in place—that's good! Building the missing elements and strengthening those you may already have will better position you for long-term success. In this book, I share insights into the respective roles of board and management, critical business processes and financial information; so that at each point of engagement between management and the board, you can fully understand one another as well as the information being discussed. As you'll see in the final step, all of these flow into the annual calendar as key elements to ensure all parties are working together against a unified plan.

Confirm the Legal Structure

This book lays out the eight steps for nonprofit boards and executives to align for success, built upon twenty-five years of my learning working within and for the nonprofit sector. My path has led me to a role on the board of Children's National Hospital, which has reinforced my learning by showing how well things can work when everything is done well, and alignment is strong. I'm honored to serve with and continue to learn from some of the best leaders in governance and management in the sector. I am starting with an overview of the legal structure because it is the foundation upon which the relationships and key responsibilities are based—it establishes the alignment of the parties. But first, let's review the history of the nonprofit sector and the types of organizations within it.

History of the Tax-Exempt Sector in the U.S.

While nonprofit activities have been around for centuries, the nonprofit sector we see today has been shaped by the tax laws that define activities and organizations exempt from income tax. Nonprofit organizations that meet certain criteria in the Internal Revenue Code are exempt from income tax for *all but unrelated business income*, though private foundations are subject to an *excise* tax on certain investment earnings. We often hear the terms nonprofit and tax-exempt used interchangeably. To understand how closely they are intertwined, let's review the history of tax-exemption in the U.S.

Charitable activity in the U.S. dates back several hundred years, prior to the establishment of a governmental framework. Early settlers formed charitable and other voluntary associations, such as hospitals, fire departments, and orphanages, to address the needs of their day. Ultimately, the young new governments developing in the U.S. would not have the capacity to address such needs. There are two types of these voluntary associations—public-serving and member-serving, categories that persist in today's nonprofit sector.

In America, communities existed before governments. There were many groups of people with a common sense of purpose and a feeling of duty to one another before there were political institutions.

Daniel Boorstin, University of Chicago Historian and 12th Librarian of Congress

When corporate income tax was first enacted in 1894, the legislation explicitly exempted "corporations, companies, or associations organized and conducted solely for charitable, religious, or educational purposes, including fraternal beneficiary associations." Building on this foundation, the Revenue Act of 1909 granted tax exemption to "any corporation or association organized and operated exclusively for religious, charitable, or educational purposes, no part of

2

the net income of which inures to the benefit of any private stockholder or individual." This clearly established that tax exemption was to be extended only to organizations expressly organized not to generate profits for owners.[2] The Revenue Act of 1913 established the foundation for the modern federal tax system. The Revenue Act of 1954 established section 501(c) of the internal revenue code, which today includes all categories of exemption except for trusts covered by IRC section 4947.

From disclosures pulled from tax filings by Cause IQ and available in the directories by category at https://www.causeiq.com/directory/, the nonprofit sector employs over 22 million people, generates $4.1 trillion in revenue and holds over $9 trillion in assets. The single largest category of nonprofits is healthcare, generating almost 50% of revenue in the sector with over 20% of total assets and over 35% of employees. Educational institutions and foundations hold a greater percentage of total assets because of endowments or foundation portfolios supporting their work. In spite of all this wide variability and the related range of constituencies served, they all share common governance requirements and the need for alignment for success.

Types of Nonprofit Organizations

There is tremendous diversity in the work performed by nonprofit organizations, their structure, how they are governed, and how they generate the resources to perform their work. Because of that, you might notice I avoid the

---

[2] A History of the Tax-Exempt Sector: An SOI Perspective by Paul Arnsberger, Melissa Ludlum, Margaret Riley, and Mark Stanton

term *nonprofit industry* and instead use the term *nonprofit sector*. In fact, there are many industries in which there are both nonprofit and for-profit entities in operation such as healthcare, education, and entertainment. In addition to these, nonprofits also serve the collective business and professional interests of entities and individuals through associations; provide human and social services; perform advocacy and community development activities; provide grants and contributions for the undertakings of public charities; serve the religious needs of parishioners of all faiths; and a range of other specific activities articulated in the Internal Revenue Code. The code sections with the greatest number of entities that fit within them are in the table below.

Code Section	Description
501(c)(3)	Religious, educational, charitable, scientific, or literary organizations, those testing for public safety, preventing cruelty to children or animals, or fostering national or international amateur sports competition. Includes public charities as well as private foundations.
501(c)(4)	Civic leagues, social welfare organizations, and local associations of employees
501(c)(5)	Labor, agriculture, and horticultural organizations
501(c)(6)	Business leagues, chambers of commerce, and real estate boards
501(c)(7)	Social and recreational clubs
501(c)(8)	Fraternal beneficiary societies and associations
501(c)(9)	Voluntary employee beneficiary associations

The list of entities exempt from tax under section 501(c)(3) is quite broad because it includes all the categories considered charitable and represents the largest number of all nonprofit organizations. It is the category for which all donations are generally deductible up to a certain percentage of an individual's income. Not all contributions to tax-exempt organizations are deductible—notably, contributions to 501(c)(4) and 501(c)(6) organizations are not eligible for charitable deduction, but in some cases can be deducted as business expenses if made for ordinary and necessary expenses related to a trade or business. The deductibility of contributions is covered in Internal Revenue Code (IRC) section 170. This classification is derived from the nature of the organization's work and thus doesn't change over time.

All 501(c)(3) organizations are classified as either a public charity or a private foundation, the determination for which is covered by IRC section 509. This distinction is important because it drives different compliance and reporting requirements and exposes the organization and its leaders to different constraints and potential fines. It's also something that can change, depending on the type of organization and level of support it receives from investments or unrelated business income; so both boards and executives should understand the criteria well in making financial decisions. Churches, schools, hospitals, certain agricultural research organizations, organizations that exclusively test for public safety, governmental entities and supporting organizations are carved out in the law and always treated as public charities. All others that are not already classified as a private foundation and have gross receipts greater than $50,000 are required to perform a public support test in Schedule A to their annual Form 990 or 990-EZ filing.

The public support test is required of an organization or community trust that:

- Operates for the benefit of a college or university owned or operated by a governmental unit;
- Normally receives a substantial part of its support from a governmental unit or from the general public; or
- Normally receives at least one-third of its support from contributions, membership fees and gross receipts from activities related to its exempt function but no more than one-third of its support from investment income or unrelated business taxable income.

I was a consultant to an organization with an affiliate that provided donations and other support for my client's program activities. That affiliate significantly reduced its fundraising activities and, within a few years, failed to meet the public support test; at which point it was reclassified as a private foundation. This exposed the organization to an excise tax on certain investment income and placed significant restrictions on transactions related to board members. In addition, the reliance on investment returns without the support of fundraising caused them to incur operating losses.

Corporate Structure

U.S. corporate law has its roots in centuries of British common law. Early corporations were formed by charters granted by the Crown to conduct commerce, like the establishment in 1600 of

East India Company to conduct trade with India. In the United States (U.S.), legislatures similarly issued charters, such as the founding in 1650 of The President and Fellows of Harvard College by the Massachusetts legislature. Indeed, the oldest universities in the U.S. were first established by state or federal legislative charters in the 1700s and early 1800s. Many storied and prestigious nonprofits such as the American Red Cross or YMCA were similarly established throughout the 1800s.

By the late 1800s, states began passing legislation to enable incorporation without legislative action. Most nonprofit organizations are now established under these state laws as nonstock corporations, which is accomplished with the filing of Articles of Incorporation, usually with the Secretary of State. The nonstock aspect to the entity reflects its nonprofit nature—there are no shares of stock which can be held by owners. Any net assets that accumulate are to be used in fulfillment of the organization's mission or, if the organization shuts down, donated to another charitable organization upon dissolution. While it's possible to organize a nonprofit as an unincorporated association—generally for smaller scale, time-limited endeavors—the corporate form provides greater liability protection and is far more prevalent.

Thirty-seven out of fifty states have modeled their nonprofit corporation statutes on the Model Nonprofit Corporation Act (MNCA) developed by the Nonprofit Organizations Committee of the Business Law Section of the American Bar Association (ABA). The remaining states follow business law in their state. The MNCA was first published in 1952, revised in 1988, followed by a third edition in 2009 and a fourth edition in 2022. These updates expanded coverage of the MNCA to include conflicts of interest, indemnification of officers and directors, the role of organizational members in decision-making, organizational member rights, board structure, electronic communications, and other technological aspects of corporate governance.

After filing of the Articles, the initial board of Directors must adopt a set of by-laws that lay out how the organization is governed. These establish the board structure and roles, director terms and manner of election, how the board operates, and the appointment and powers of a chief executive. If there are organizational members, by-laws will usually specify the organizational members or describe how organizational members are admitted to the membership and how the organizational members conduct business. To the extent not covered in the Articles, the by-laws may indicate what powers are reserved to the organizational members. By their nature and as articulated in the Articles and By-Laws, nonstock corporations vest the control and oversight of the organization in the board or between the board and organizational member(s). If there are organizational members, the entity will have interaction between and among each of the three groups, and if there are no organizational members, then authority and responsibilities are allocated between the board and chief executive as shown in the graphic below. Whether the corporation has organizational members or not is usually clearly articulated in the Articles of Incorporation.

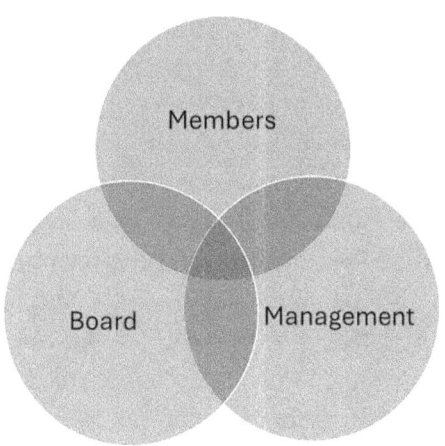

Articles of Incorporation

The Articles must include certain basic elements to meet the minimum requirements for incorporation. While there may be some variation from state to state, in general all articles need to cover the following areas:

- Corporation name
- Duration (often perpetual, but may be time-limited)
- Principal place of business
- Purpose(s)
- Powers
- Organizational membership (if any)
- Board of Directors
- Powers reserved
- Registered office/agent
- Initial directors
- Incorporators

As you review the Articles for your organization, you should focus particularly on purposes, powers, organizational membership, and any powers reserved. I'll discuss each of those in more detail below.

The section for *purpose(s)* is where one lists the charitable purposes for which the corporation is being formed, and language is usually tied—at least minimally—into the purposes for which exemption is available in the Internal Revenue Code. These may be specific to the organization's targeted population, such as "to organize and carry on charitable, educational, and social activities for the Spanish-speaking residents of the State." These may also explicitly address some of the other tax related criteria, such as "the Corporation is operated exclusively for nonprofit purposes and no part of the income or assets of the Corporation shall be distributed to nor inure to the benefit of any individual."

Powers are frequently broad-based and may include language such as "the corporation is empowered to receive property by grant, contract or otherwise from the government of the United States, any state or local government and any charitable or educational organization (including foundations)." This section may also clarify that the organization "is empowered to buy, own, sell, assign, mortgage or lease any real estate and personal property; borrow money and issue evidence of indebtedness; and to perform all acts reasonably necessary to accomplish the purpose of the Corporation."

The section on *organizational membership* is pivotal. If there are no organizational members, there is usually a section explicitly saying there are no such members. Unless the organization is an association of professional or business interests, the number of organizational members may be stated. A limited number of one or a few organizational members may be used as an element of control by incorporators to ensure the corporation stays true to its mission, or if the organizational members are other corporations, stays true to the purpose of the entity as part of a group of entities.

Powers reserved, if any are stated, are critical constraints placed on who has authority to take enumerated acts. It may hold that, if there are organizational members, the organizational members retain the power to approve borrowing, the purchase of real estate, and even to select or approve the independent auditors. Arguably, the most significant power that may be reserved to the organizational members is the election and removal of members of the Board of Directors. If that language is present, then organizational members ultimately control the organization.

There are three duties of board members established in the laws under which organizations are incorporated:

- **Duty of Care:** Board members must perform their roles with the care an ordinary and prudent person would use, including active participation, familiarizing themselves with the work, and carefully evaluating information provided to them.
- **Duty of Loyalty:** Board members must place the interests of the organization and public served above their own personal interests in discharging their responsibilities.
- **Duty of Obedience:** Board members must work to ensure the organization complies with all applicable laws, reporting requirements, and its own by-laws and articles of incorporation.

While the Articles of Incorporation establish the entity in very basic terms, the by-laws are required to put structure to how the entity will function.

By-Laws

While Articles of Incorporation are frequently brief, just a few pages, many By-Laws are extensive and can range dozens of pages; because they cover much more detail about the way governance of the entity will operate. They will provide extensive detail on the operation of the board, and of the organizational membership, if there are organizational members. They will describe how the board relates to and directs the management of the corporation. I would encourage those not in board roles to nonetheless gain an understanding of some of these key provisions and look for them in your own corporation's by-laws. They will help management understand how the board and organizational members operate so they can understand how best to interact with each group of stakeholders.

- **Organizational Membership**: The by-laws will address whether there are organizational members, and if so, either name them or describe eligibility and criteria for admission. Whether the organizational members are named or described, many other characteristics of organizational members are then covered—powers and authority, dues, meetings and other official actions, removal, and reinstatement. Later in the chapter, we'll discuss how complex the organizational structure can be with organizational members involved.

- **Board of Directors Structure**: By-laws will specify the number of directors, usually expressed as a range and sometimes with a minimum threshold (e.g. "not less than seven nor more than fifteen" directors) as well as how they are selected and their term of office. They will also define the roles of officers of the board, how they are selected and their term of office. These will usually include a Chair (or President), Vice Chair (or Vice President), Secretary and Treasurer. Their responsibilities and authority are usually defined as well, such as the Chair having the authority to call meetings, set the agenda, serve ex officio on all committees, or lead the Executive Committee. Treasurers sometimes also serve as the chair of the Finance Committee.

- **Committees**: By-laws will describe any standing committees, which frequently include an executive committee, governance committee, finance committee, and audit committee. There will also be information on the number of committee members, how they are selected and how long they serve; as well as the focus of each committee, the authorities granted to each committee, and how the chair is appointed or selected. We'll discuss committees in greater detail in the next chapter on board and management roles because the committees are where the greatest interaction between the broader management team and board members occurs. There may be provisions for the creation of ad hoc committees as well.

- **Meetings**: The by-laws will prescribe the minimum number of meetings to be held each year and may designate one of the meetings as an Annual Meeting, at which specific actions such as electing new board members, renewing terms of existing members, and voting on the slate of board officers is to take place. There will be provisions for how meetings are called (e.g. they may require a specific number of days of notice and may expressly allow telephonic or virtual meetings). These provisions are important for management to understand if they need to get information before the board for specific actions needed.

- **Executive and staff:** By-laws will usually indicate that the Board will select a chief executive, who will then be responsible for the day-to-day activities of the organization and that the chief executive may employ staff, name vice presidents, or put other structures in place, to perform the work of the organization. This is where the distinct roles of management and the board are most clear. While the board is charged with overseeing many aspects of the corporation, they do so at a policy, planning and resource allocation level but explicitly hire a chief executive to implement the work.

The bulk of misalignment and conflict between boards, executives and management teams is rooted in misunderstanding the distinction between the governance role of the board and the operational and day to day management roles of the executive and their staff. Over half of the boards on which I've served or interacted with have struggled with this challenge at one point or another. This is why Step 1 in this chapter and the following Step 2 of the process are necessary, indeed critical. The misunderstanding often plays out with board members who second guess management decisions and derail the focus of the board from higher-level strategic issues, miring discussions in reviews of management decisions and weighing alternatives. Board education is important, and at times changes to board composition may be necessary to ensure the right people are in the right roles.

Unless an organization is led by volunteers, best practice is for the chief executive to hold the title of President because, under state law, this role has specific responsibilities and authority. Board members generally have no individual authority, so having the chair of the board serve as President vests them with individual authority and thus exposes them to liability. Specifically, state laws and regulations often require whoever holds the President title to sign certain documents. Executing and attesting to programmatic, financial, and compliance related documents is a management function, so having a board member in the role required to sign blurs the line between governance and management. In addition, most board members do not have expertise in the operations of the organization to fully understand what is being reported and to which they must attest, often under penalty of perjury. Because the environment in which nonprofits operate can be dynamic, best practices may evolve, and specific business needs may emerge, by-laws should be updated as needed to ensure the structure is responsive.

As a board chair, I've worked closely with outside counsel to understand the various provisions of by-laws and, in several instances, worked with them to update them. For one organization, we added the President title to the chief executive precisely because of the issues described above, resulting in Chair and Vice Chair roles on the board with a President and CEO as the chief staff officer. For other organizations, we've adjusted the number of board members or board meetings required to provide more flexibility as we navigated significant governance transitions. By-laws should describe the process to amend them, usually requiring a board vote, but if there are organizational members in the corporate structure, the organizational members may be required to vote on adoption of any amendments. The changes I described above were presented to and discussed with the full board prior to a vote and, in the case of the title changes, we asked outside counsel to be present to discuss the changes and governance best practices to provide context for the board before the vote was taken.

Organizational Membership Structures

State laws treat organizational members like stockholders. Stock represents both a financial interest and an element of control in a for-profit corporation, but nonprofit corporations are created as nonstock corporations, because there can be no individual financial interests. Voting rights are allocated to organizational members similar to voting rights held by shareholders. Nonstock corporations with organizational members may have one or more organizational members and may also have one or more classes of membership. Organizational members may be assessed dues, fees or other charges to the extent outlined in the Articles or by-laws. Generally, different classes of organizational membership may be treated differently within the constraints set out in the Articles or by-laws, including that certain classes of membership may be explicitly exempted from paying dues, fees or other assessments. Organizational membership may be subject to termination and reinstatement as provided in the by-laws.

Associations that serve business or professional interests are often structured so that organizational members participate in governance. They may elect new board members, vote on the slate of board officers, approve any changes to the by-laws, approve the annual budget or major expenditures, approve changes to dues or fees, approve policies, and perhaps approve a dissolution of the entity. While this may seem unwieldy, associations are by design created to serve the organizational members and the larger this membership, the more precise the by-laws should be. The chief executive, often with an Executive Director title, is usually selected by and reports to the board.

The by-laws of such associations often have more complex structures for organizational members than the board of directors. Organizational members may come from different types of businesses or organizations within an industry, perhaps with individual professional members, as well as corporate members. The dues structures may vary, and each group may have different levels of representation on the board, enforced through a specific number of seats for each type of organizational membership.

I watched association dynamics at play early in my consulting career when my firm proposed an engagement to assist the association with its accounting function. In that case, the organizational members reserved the authority to enter into significant contractual commitments such as what we proposed, so after making our presentation to the Board, they then took the recommendation to the organizational members at their annual meeting in order to secure authorization to execute a contract. Unfortunately, the organizational members felt they were not given sufficient time or information to evaluate the contract and weren't comfortable with the dollar value, so they declined to move forward and directed the board to pursue other options.

An organizational member structure can also be used for nonprofits that are *not* associations. In such cases, there may be a single organizational member, which is most often used to secure control over a subsidiary by requiring approval by the organizational member for any additions to the board, the selection of a chief executive, or changes to by-laws. This is a structure that is available under the law in part because there is no stock and there is no other way to ensure control over a subsidiary. This structure can also be leveraged in a multi-entity environment, so that subsidiary entities have the parent as the sole organizational member and thus the parent board can exercise control over the group of entities. In such a structure, the organizational member may have other powers reserved to it, such as the approval of a sale of assets or dissolution. It is useful for board members and management to understand this critical aspect of the legal structure. It clarifies where and how power is held over the conduct of corporate affairs.

These structural choices enable nonprofits to organize themselves in ways that vest control in the parties who are most likely to hew closely to the mission of the organization. A single-member nonstock nonprofit corporation could be structured to concentrate control and only delegate to the board or management those authorities that make the most sense in the circumstances. Religious-affiliated organizations will often name a common leadership role or entity within the church structure as an organizational member.

I have seen instances in which the incorporators failed to anticipate the loss of control—they relied on the by-laws to name the leader of the "sponsoring" organization as chair. Unfortunately, the chair is just one vote. The by-laws provided that the by-laws could be amended by a majority vote of the board, and the other board members amended the by-laws to remove that provision. Control in that case could have been accomplished by reserving to an organizational member the approval of any by-law changes and assigning that member role to the leader of the sponsoring organization.

While this may sound fairly complicated and dry, many people are exposed to, perhaps, the most local of nonprofit organizations—homeowners, condominium, or cooperative associations. As reported by the Community Association Institute, in 2020 there were over 70 million residents living in over 350,000 communities with a community association. Organizational membership is usually tied to the deed to a property, which enables the owner to vote on members of the board and, perhaps, other changes. Organizational membership is usually closed to those with an organizational membership interest carried by the deed; organizational membership with associated rights transfer with the property and are not retained by an organizational member who no longer owns the related property. In my neighborhood, the board also hires a manager to handle day-to-day activities, including billing, vendor coordination, mailing to new organizational members when properties transfer, and other functions. In these smaller, localized organizations, the directors may function more in a managerial manner because they tend to limit expenditure on staff or management contracts. Volunteers, both on the board or appointed by the board, may coordinate common area maintenance, newsletters, finance, government relations, and community events.

Key Points from the Legal Structure

I've reviewed a lot of information with you about the way Articles of Incorporation and By-Laws define the structure of governance and operationalize management for any given nonprofit organization structured as a nonstock corporation.

There are important implications of these nonstock corporation structures:

- Corporations with organizational members will likely allocate governance authority between organizational members and the board of directors.

- Organizational members have authority as a body; individual organizational members have any voting power granted to them in the organizing documents.

- Boards have authority as a body; individual directors have the power of a vote, but have no other individual authority or power except as it relates to the conduct of the board.

- Boards select and oversee a chief executive, who is responsible for overseeing day-to-day operations and any personnel hired to perform the work of the organization.

- Management teams are appointed by and accountable to the chief executive; neither individual organizational members nor individual directors have authority to direct management or staff.

The by-laws also define how the board conducts its activities:

- A chair coordinates the activities of the board within the constraints described in the organizing documents.
- Much of the work of the board is allocated to committees, who provide more direct oversight of management activities.

The legal structure sets the boundaries. In the next chapter, we'll review the day-to-day relationships between the board, executive and management within the constraints of this foundation.

Clarify Roles and Responsibilities

Attending your first board meeting is somewhat like the first day at a new school when you were growing up. When you look around the room, you see a group of individuals with whom you'll spend a fair amount of time in the coming years but are unsure of the norms, with whom you'll click or quite where this experience will take you. Hopefully, your experience with the board, either as a director or a member of management, will be less traumatic than your school-age experience!

In that initial meeting, staff or managers may have had little preparation for what to expect, what their responsibilities are, or how they should interact. New board members may have had introductory discussions with the staff supporting the board, the CEO and Chair or head of the nominating or governance committee. Over the past twenty years, I've seen a range of practices from little to no effort at onboarding in some instances, to robust onboarding in other instances—but in no case have I seen any material explicitly address the relationship between the board, the chief executive, management, and staff.

As with many employers, nonprofit organizations generally recognize the need to support the learning curve for incoming employees by having a structured onboarding process. They provide background information relevant to the job and may assign a buddy. For employees who are likely to support the flow of information to the board, it would be extremely useful to include information about the board and how it interacts with their function, so that they have a foundation for future activity with the board. Interaction with and support for the board should also be incorporated into position descriptions where appropriate.

Nonprofits are beginning to recognize the need to have an appropriate onboarding program for new board members as well, which is an investment that enables the board to quickly integrate new members into governance. While onboarding for board members usually includes by-laws, tax returns, any strategic plans, and the annual budget, more information is needed on roles and responsibilities. New board members should receive information on the board's role and how it relates to the chief executive, to management and to staff. I served on one board that assigned a fellow director as a buddy to new members, which was both well received and resulted in faster attainment of cohesion as a board. Some nonprofits now embrace position descriptions for board members, which I'd strongly recommend.

In my experience, severely limiting board interaction with management and staff can lead to unhealthy assumptions by staff that the board is disconnected from the work, doesn't value the staff, and makes decisions without knowing what is going on within the organization. Receiving everything through the filter of the chief executive should be a red flag to the board. In the other extreme, though, it is possible board members can have extensive interaction with staff outside the boardroom, perhaps while serving as volunteers in the programs—that can cloud boundaries and lead to staff involving the board in day-to-day management issues. The board, chief executive, management, and staff each have complementary and distinct responsibilities in the functioning of a nonprofit organization that should be documented and understood by all parties.

Challenges with clarity of roles can plague organizations large and small, though they play out in different ways. Boards of larger, established organizations with full management teams in place should honor the boundaries between board and management roles, in large part because stepping into a management role or attempting to direct staff undermines the authority and effectiveness of the chief executive. It's hard for the board to hold a chief executive accountable if the board goes around the executive to direct staff or impose management decisions.

Newer, smaller organizations, though, may need help from the board to support certain functions like accounting, marketing, or technology, for example. In such cases, the board members providing that support need to be careful to provide the help but maintain the boundaries. Remember that individual board members have no authority on their own, and they are largely serving in a support role, so any observations or feedback from the support they provide should be shared in a collaborative and constructive manner. I worked with a client who was launching a new organization, so their board was actively involved in the early days. While there were some early challenges in maintaining the boundaries, their job was to ensure the executive had the tools needed to successfully launch the organization and allow the executive to take those functions into the management team, as the resources could be hired. They can then judge the performance of the executive after being given the tools. This was a success story, but it required great trust and diplomacy to navigate those early days.

Authority and Reporting Lines

The board is responsible for governance, which is derived from the Greek verb kubernaein, which means "to steer." In the corporate context, it is the process of overseeing the control and direction of the entity—steering the organization. The chief executive is responsible for the day-to-day management of the organization. The word 'management' is derived from the Latin noun *manus*, which means "hand." In the corporate context, it is the process through which the activities of the organization are implemented—the hands-on activity of performing the work. The chief executive is usually the only person formally reporting directly to the board, and is delegated specific authority in the by-laws or as otherwise directed by the board. It is the chief executive who will determine the staff and management structure they need to effectively implement the work. All management and staff report through the management structure to the chief executive—the board has no direct authority over individual employees other than the chief executive.

Recall that board members hold power and have authority as a group, not individually. No one board member can direct the chief executive or anyone reporting to the chief executive. The board cannot, as a body or individually, direct staff in any way. Later, we'll discuss the extensive interaction between the board and management or staff through committee work, where the board may make requests of staff, but it is the chief executive's prerogative whether the work is to be performed by that individual or someone else as well as to negotiate with the board the scope and timelines for the request. After all, the board can't hold the chief executive accountable if they interfere by setting priorities for the management team reporting to the executive. The chief executive remains accountable to the board for overall performance, so if the board has a concern about any choices made that they feel may be undermining the chief executive's effectiveness, they can decide whether and how to raise them, but that determination should be made by the board as a whole, not by an individual board member.

I'll discuss the operation of the board later in this chapter, but the one role that is particularly relevant to this discussion is the chair. The chair's sole authority as an individual member is that granted in the by-laws, which is generally to manage the board's process within the constraints of the by-laws. The position has no direct authority over the chief executive, management, or staff. The chair, nonetheless, usually spends far more time with the chief executive than anyone else, in part because of the chair's role in managing the board's process and in part because the chair can help the executive think through challenges and weigh courses of action. In my various stints as chair, I met either bi-weekly or monthly with the chief executive, though bi-weekly keeps us more in sync. It also ensures if we miss a meeting because of travel or conflicts, we still meet frequently enough.

Those meetings or calls were used to keep me up to date on issues, so I could determine when the board might need to be notified of something between meetings, if a special meeting of the board should be called, or otherwise to plan the details for upcoming board meetings. As a visible representative of the board, the chair may sign cover letters in annual reports or letters to donors, may appear at public events, and may meet with donors—I've done all of those things as chair.

I was serving as chair of a board that struggled with the information being presented to it by the chief financial officer, who was serving in a dual role as both the chief financial officer and chief operating officer. The choice to combine the two roles was made by the chief executive, and the board felt it was a poor decision based on the quality of information and results we were seeing. The board correctly avoided specifically directing the COO/CFO to address the concerns arising from the joint role or the gaps in information and instead communicated the concerns to the chief executive, who will be judged on their ability to structure the management team effectively to manage and control risk, while also providing sufficient transparency through reporting to the board.

In one of my stints as a board chair, the chief executive would occasionally, I hoped jokingly, call me "the boss." My legal authority on the board was limited, though through my tenure I had earned some credibility and trust, so I was listened to on matters before the board. At the end of the day, the chief executive was still accountable to the full board and my role was primarily to set the agenda for, call, and lead meetings.

There is one circumstance in which the chair could be the boss, and that's when the chief executive also serves as chair. While this has been a practice on some for-profit boards, it is rare in the nonprofit sector. Business leaders and academics are also raising alarms about its continued practice in the for-profit sector.[3] It sets up an impossible conflict in which the person who leads the body that oversees the CEO is… the CEO. In addition to that troubling conflict, the organization misses the value that another leader with separate experiences and insights can contribute to an independent chair role.

Similar to a *powers reserved* clause in the Articles of Incorporation, there may be a powers reserved clause in the By-Laws that constrains the chief executive. These might include whether to buy or sell property, take on debt, or similar "big decisions." The board can easily adopt a resolution to grant authority to the chief executive for any individual transaction, but the extra layer of scrutiny before a momentous decision can be made is a safeguard. As a reminder, the Articles or by-laws may also reserve certain powers to organizational members, if there are such members.

As I'll discuss later, the board may have extensive interaction with some management and staff because it needs information they possess to discharge its duties, particularly in committee work, which I'll discuss later in this chapter. If board members have any observations about individual performance, they should share it with the chief executive without judgment. For board members reading this, it is important to remember that the board has no idea what level of resources the manager has been afforded to complete their work, whether they are matrixed with another team and there were breakdowns in the flow of information between the teams, or if they are working through challenges on their own team. Only the chief executive

---

[3] https://hbr.org/2020/03/why-the-ceo-shouldnt-also-be-the-board-chair

will have the relevant information to determine whether they need to coach a manager on their performance, adjust resources, realign teams, or take other actions. The board owes it to the organization and the chief executive to share their observations and leave any follow-up to the chief executive. The board needs to build a collaborative relationship with the chief executive and give them the space to work through management issues and prioritize where attention is most needed.

When I joined one of the boards on which I served, their structure had a built-in succession in which the Vice Chair would become the Chair after two years. I initially ascended to the Chair role through this structure and generally thought it was fine. After we hired a new CEO, though, and nearing a transition when the Vice Chair would have ascended to the Chair, the Vice Chair began actively undermining the new CEO. It created unacceptable tension between the board and CEO, so I spoke to the rest of the board to see if they agreed with me and would be willing to vote for the removal of the Vice Chair. They agreed, I conveyed that to the Vice Chair and requested his resignation, which was given. We then amended the by-laws to make the Chair and Vice Chair distinct roles, with each voted upon separately with no predetermined succession.

One last note on authority and reporting lines—board members should have no role in personnel matters, and should any staff raise concerns about personnel other than the chief executive, they should be referred to the human resources function or, if appropriate, a whistleblower hotline. Any statement a board member makes about personnel could expose the organization to risk and undermine the authority and effectiveness of the chief executive. If there are concerns raised about the chief executive, no individual board member should engage directly, and the board should discuss as a group. Unfortunately, I've occasionally received letters from employees or members of the public about staff or a chief executive—and usually they write to multiple board members. All matters about the staff should be referred to the chief executive. The board should collectively evaluate any concerns about the chief executive, gathering input from the executive, if appropriate.

If the concerns regarding the executive warrant it, the board should consider an investigation led by an independent party where possible. In most cases, as board chair I had direct access to inside or outside counsel we would use for board matters, such as updates to by-laws, drafting agreements with the executive, and other contractual issues, so I would consult them for help if needed. When an investigation is required, it can be one of the most unfortunate and difficult times for an organization and its leadership. All parties need to exercise utmost discretion regardless of the outcome, so that the work and the reputation of the organization is not damaged. If separation of an executive is needed, that too should be handled with great care.

Board members also fulfill an advisory role, which is not one in which they have authority, but instead one that is to serve as a support to the chief executive and management team. Their diverse backgrounds bring critical advisory support to the organization, as well as relationships within the community that strengthen the organization's connections and thus capability to have significant impact.

Board Member Exposure to Programs

Board members who have not seen the work of the organization in action often have difficulty relating to the issues or conditions they hear about in board or committee meetings. The duty of care requires them to familiarize themselves with the work of the organization, to ensure they have sufficient information and perspective to ground any actions or decisions made by the board. While board members may not have a professional or personal connection to the work, they need to be able to observe and ask questions to ensure they understand the work for which they are accountable. Some boards accomplish this by bringing program leaders into board meetings to discuss their work in the form of a "mission moment."

At times, it might be appropriate and more impactful for board members to visit program sites— this in largely controlled ways. Board member involvement shouldn't be disruptive to program activities and should be supported with staff or a manager who can escort a board member during the program visit to both facilitate interaction with staff and field questions from the board member who is learning important aspects of the work. While a board member is on such a visit, they should be mindful of the boundaries and follow the direction of their escort without attempting to direct the staff in any way. If they have any questions about the performance of their escort or any of the staff they observe, they should speak separately with the chief executive. Board members may not understand how the service is delivered or what the staff member's role is in the work. It is also completely up to the chief executive to determine whether any follow-up is required.

The visit can be as important for staff and managers as it is for board members. I visited programs in numerous instances as a board chair. I participated in a Thanksgiving visit to a group home with the CEO and development staff, joined a tour being given to a potential funder and participated in a visit by a foreign dignitary, who was a champion for similar programming in their home country. In each case, staff and managers had an opportunity to showcase their work, share their experience, teach me about best practices, and be recognized for their contributions. Along with other board members, I've toured new facilities, received presentations from service recipients, and met with strategic partners. These experiences also prepare board members with perspectives that enable them to be better ambassadors in the community.

Staff should know that board members share their commitment to the mission and may have even been touched by the work they do in one way or another. They also bring diverse backgrounds to their role—from marketing, engineering, technology, financial services, professional services, consumer products, retail, and many other industries, as well as from other nonprofits—that can improve the agility and responsiveness of the organization in meeting the needs of the community it serves. Staff should expect that some board members may not be familiar with the specific elements of the work they do beyond the mission and the impact they have, and any issues they have with how they are managed should be raised with management. If they need to raise concerns about unethical or dangerous behavior, they should follow the whistleblowing guidelines set out for the organization.

Board members should know that program and administrative staff, managers and senior leaders may have specialization in their areas of responsibility, but not have a complete understanding of how your roles and theirs relate to one another in the overall functioning of the organization. If you observe their work, you may not have the context for what you are seeing at the moment so you should note to yourself to ask questions later, to better understand the work, but do not try to intercede. If they are able, they will describe the work to you at the time.

Committee Work by Board and Staff Support

The board conducts much of its work through committees, working closely with management and staff who provide information that helps the board monitor financial and operational performance, as well as compliance and achievement of strategic priorities. The by-laws will specify the standing committees that should be aligned with the management team to ensure proper communication and flow of information to the board.

Committees should adopt and annually review charters that lay out their responsibilities, work process, and the information they require from management to aid them in discharging their duties. For instance, the Finance Committee charter may indicate that the committee will review quarterly financial statements in a certain format, therefore management is clear on deliverables required and at what frequency. I've reviewed some charters that fell out of date, including functions that didn't exist in the organization—in one case, the audit committee charter referred to an internal audit function that was never in place. It is important to review charters annually, ideally at the first meeting of each new year.

The board should actively maintain key standing committees as well as occasionally empanel ad hoc committees for specific needs such as a new CEO selection or triennial strategic planning process. Traditionally, there are three committees through which the board fulfills many of its responsibilities— Finance Committee, Audit, Risk and Compliance Committee, and Governance Committee. It is through these committees that management engages most directly with the board.

Finance Committee: Given the challenging environment in which many nonprofits operate, this is a critical committee that should have board directors who have sufficient business acumen to understand the information being discussed. The chief financial officer and controller are the key staff liaisons with this committee. This committee should be involved on the front-end in planning and budgeting and, on the back end, measuring performance against budget. In understanding performance, however, additional analysis, metrics and trending may be needed. All financial reporting and budget discussions should go through this committee. I'll review the planning process in more detail in a later chapter. The important point here is that through the finance committee, the board and management should have robust dialogue about financial matters throughout the year and in preparation for each new fiscal year.

Audit, Risk and Compliance Committee: At a very high level, this committee is usually charged with selecting and overseeing the work of external auditors, receiving reports directly from an in-house or otherwise sourced internal audit function, and overseeing overall compliance and risk management, which is a key accountability of a board. This committee, perhaps more than any other, reviews information from outside advisers such as auditors about management and organizational performance. We'll discuss the work of this committee in much greater detail in Step 4.

Governance Committee: This committee may include "nominating" in the name or not, but is frequently responsible for coordinating the planning for and screening of new board members. Management may help identify candidates; allowing the CEO to identify relationships they hold—which could benefit the organization—should be considered as well. I've served with board members brought on because of connections with the chief executive who were fully objective with respect to the performance of the chief executive. Board members screened for character and objectivity with clarity about the role are positioned to perform the role well.

A note on committees, advisory boards, or subsidiary boards – making sure there is important work to be done at each level, with members that are engaged and appropriate to the work is critical. Each group requires staff support to be meaningful, and it can be a drain on management resources to support too many governance structures.

Operation of the Board

Boards are structured with several formal roles—chair, vice chair, secretary, and treasurer. In these roles, directors are fulfilling board functions. The secretary is responsible for corporate records, the treasurer is responsible for ensuring there are financial records and controls overall, and the chair/vice chair are responsible for coordinating and leading the board functions—meetings, governance, specific roles outlined in the by-laws. Being a board leader does not give a director any individual authority outside of the board.

Within a broad range, some boards retain open seats for a variety of reasons, and boards should be opportunistic in recruiting new members for those vacancies. The board may seek someone with a specific professional background, who represents the community served, or has other characteristics. They may also fill a board seat with a representative of another organization with which they partner in service delivery.

While we discussed the focus of some key standing committees earlier, the by-laws will specify what standing committees must be maintained, the required composition of those committees and how members are appointed or elected.

State law requires boards to document their proceedings by keeping minutes and these minutes become part of the corporate record. Some state laws will prescribe certain committee structures that must be in place, the criteria for membership, and the authority of the committees. Many state laws exempt volunteer board members from liability in discharging their responsibilities to the extent they seek and receive advice from professionals in various areas of oversight.

Boards should reflect on their effectiveness and individual board members should be able to appraise their own performance against expectations. The position description will enable better dialogues between the chair and individual board members as part of an annual assessment process.

So how does a board develop a strong collaborative relationship with the leadership team that is respectful of the legal boundaries? There are four key elements:

- **Onboarding:** The board should have an onboarding process for new members that includes giving them copies of the articles of incorporation, by-laws, recent audit reports, recent tax filings, recent program reports, and any significant press or other publicly distributed information.

- **Charter:** Each committee should have a charter that clarifies how the committee will conduct its work, any policies guiding the work of the committee (e.g. an investment policy), what information will be provided by management, at what frequency and in what form.

- **Calendar:** The board should establish a board calendar to ensure key board activities are distributed throughout the year, including appropriate program updates and board education, to ensure management can anticipate and prepare information for each meeting.

- **Goals:** Set clear measurable goals to help the chief executive to focus effort on key strategic and operational priorities. These should include not just areas the chief executive will do on their own but also goals that should likely require work through key direct reports

I've served on and worked with boards that failed to engage in constructive goal setting with the chief executive or failed to evaluate their performance on a regular basis. Those are some of the most effective mechanisms to build a relationship between the board and chief executive. Relationships are healthiest when expectations are clear, feedback is fair and honest, and goals that help move the organization to a new level of performance are set. Goals set with the executive then help the executive set goals with their management teams and desired outcomes can be achieved. In one instance, the chief executive negotiated a provision in their contract that absent an annual review they would receive an automatic pay increase, and that eventually got the attention of the board. True alignment requires trust and transparency.

> "Coming together is a beginning, staying together is progress, and working together is success."
>
> *Henry Ford*

A Special Note on Times of Leadership Transition

Transition to a new chief executive is a challenge for management, to be sure. The incoming chief executive must assess what they need in a management team in the context of the institution at the time they arrive. That may require changes in management structure, the elimination of some roles and the creation of others. As we described in the discussion of by-laws, the chief executive is vested with the authority to determine organizational structure and determine what positions will be needed to effectively manage the organization. This usually takes time for chief executives new to an organization.

The one time I was appointed CEO of a nonprofit, I was an internal candidate moving up from the CFO role I held for several years. I therefore had the benefit of knowing most of the organization well, and even had some input into shaping it. I fairly quickly exercised my authority to make a few limited changes in management structure and composition to best position the organization for success under my leadership. Though I kept the board informed of the changes, it was within my purview to make them.

As a board member, I've assisted and observed several incoming chief executives navigate their role. A high-quality search process is critical in ensuring the relationship starts off well. The selection of a new chief executive is one of the most important tasks of a board, and how the board handles the process is observed by the management team that will report to the new executive. I've participated as a board member in the selection of a new chief executive three times using a formal search process (once as Chair) and three times in appointing an interim chief executive (twice as Chair). As a consultant, I've supported two searches as the Finance point of contact, providing information to the search firms and candidates.

The best example of board leadership I ever saw in a board chair—not me but someone from whom I learned a great deal—was in the selection of a new CEO. The Chair never put their thumb on the scale, but created an environment in which all opinions and concerns were aired during our deliberations. The Chair organized the board's engagement in the process, to ensure all finalists brought forward by the search committee were given ample opportunity to interact with board members and be given a chance to present their vision to the board. I was passionate about the selection and was given the space to share my observation without judgment or undue limitation. To this day, we'll never know whether the Chair had a preference because in that space, their role was to facilitate the board process and support both the board and the selected executive. It was for me, a masterclass in leadership.

Key Points about Roles and Responsibilities

We have now identified how to structure board and management interaction working within the constraints of the authority and conduct articulated in a nonprofit's organizing documents. As we move into later chapters, please remember these key points:

- The board is *accountable* for the functioning of the organization and its effectiveness in fulfilling its mission; management is largely *responsible* for delivering on the same goals.
- The board and management have complementary roles, with the chief executive guiding management's execution and the board providing oversight to ensure delivery.
- The quality of information that management shares with the board is essential to keeping the organization on track and enabling the board to make appropriate strategic adjustments as needed.

STEP 3

Gain a Shared Understanding
of the Financial Statements

I began performing accounting functions for a nonprofit organization in 1983 while in college and have been producing financial statements and financial reports for more than 40 years. During that time, accounting systems and analytical tools have significantly improved, enabling more robust and useful financial reporting and analysis. The internal and external financial statements and reports that the organization produces are among the key mechanisms by which the board oversees management performance, weighs the organization's effectiveness, and monitors financial risk. It is therefore critical that both the board and management have a shared understanding of the information and how to interpret it. Financial reporting standards for nonprofit organizations have evolved over the years and today provide more comparability than ever before.

There are two broad categories of stakeholders for nonprofit financial reporting—those within the organization and those outside the organization, each of whom have unique needs for financial information. Internal stakeholders primarily need financial management reports and budget versus actual reports, to monitor financial performance against approved budgets at the departmental and organizational level as well as for specific programs and grants. External stakeholders use financial reporting to understand and monitor the overall financial health and sustainability of organizations as well as monitor compliance with key financial performance metrics. External financial reporting is prescribed by accounting standards promulgated by the Financial Accounting Standards Board (FASB), while internal financial reports are highly customized to the unique aspects of an organization's work— we will discuss them later in the chapter.

The most consistent gap I've encountered coming into consulting engagements with boards and management teams over the past twenty years has been a lack of understandable, timely, and reliable financial reporting. After spending time understanding their needs and the information available, I've enhanced reporting and how it is presented to ensure both the board and management have a full and consistent understanding of the information. The boards and management teams with whom I've worked this way often share that they understand the information fully for the first time. Because this is such a persistent issue, ensuring boards and management teams have a shared understanding of financial statements is a critical need in achieving alignment.

External Financial Statements

Since these are often only produced annually, board members and management are less familiar with the presentation than they are with the internal financial reports by which they monitor performance throughout the year. Though they may be less familiar, these statements present the organization's financial results to outside stakeholders. Organizations that are subject to single audit requirements will have their full set of audited financial statements publicly available in the single audit clearinghouse.[4] All boards, chief executives, and management teams should learn how their results will appear in these financial statements and have their budget prepared in a consistent format so they know how the results would appear to outsiders at the end of the year when they approve the budget.

An organization's published audited or reviewed financial statements, either of which should have a set of the basic financial statements and accompanying notes, are the most comprehensive yet high-level view of the financial position and results of the organization. They include detailed notes describing the organization, its activities, the application of accounting principles, and additional information about key amounts on the financial statements. Management is responsible for the preparation of these financial statements and an independent accounting firm may perform an audit or review of the financial statements and will issue an audit or review report following their work.

Financial statements were not as broadly comparable as they have been since June 1993, when the FASB issued two Statements of Financial Accounting Standards (SFASs) – No.

---

[4]   Under Uniform Guidance issued by the U.S. Government's Office of Management and Budget, the threshold has been $750,000 of expenditures of federal awards in a fiscal year since 2015. That threshold will increase to $1,000,000 effective October 1, 2024, with agency-specific implementation guidance yet to be released.

116, *Accounting for Contributions Received and Contributions Made*, and No. 117, *Financial Statements for Nonprofit Organizations*. These statements gave clear guidance on when contributions made or received were recognized, introduced three classes of net assets—unrestricted, temporarily restricted, and permanently restricted—and standardized reporting for all nonprofit organizations to provide a consistent presentation and make financial information more comparable from one entity to the next. These standards have been refined over the past thirty years, but fundamental principles have remained intact. In 2008, the FASB reorganized accounting standards into the Accounting Standards Codification (ASC), which has grouped the standards into meaningful categories. Nonprofit financial statements are now covered in ASC 958. The ASC collectively articulates accounting principles generally accepted in the United States (U.S. GAAP) that are referred to in auditors' reports and notes to financial statements.

Under U.S. GAAP, the basic financial statements for a nonprofit include the Statement of Financial Position, Statement of Activities and Statement of Cash Flows. These are similar to commercial statements with some critical reporting and structural differences. The corresponding commercial statements are shown in the table below.

Nonprofit Sector Term	Commercial Sector Term
Statement of Financial Position	Balance Sheet
Statement of Activities	Income Statement
Statement of Cash Flows	Statement of Cash Flows

The size of an organization doesn't dictate the complexity of the financial statements, instead the nature of the work and funding sources will have a more determinative effect. A complete set of audited financial statements for a private foundation with $69 billion in assets can be 20 pages, including the auditor's report, financial statements, and notes. A hospital with $2.5 billion in assets can have a set of audited financial statements that is 42 pages. I'll now walk you through each of these basic financial statements.

I've worked with several clients to update their financial statements as circumstances change or to better reflect the work after years of just rolling forward the same formats. While the structure and required elements of external financial statements are prescribed, the content should reflect the organization and its work. Auditors may provide guidance on language for how accounting standards are applied or policies are articulated to demonstrate compliance with the standards, but management should make sure the notes clearly describe the work and circumstances. Even the groupings within the basic financial statements should be reviewed periodically and updated where appropriate to better reflect the financial position or activities of the organization.

Statement of Financial Position

The name of this statement is apt, providing a clear understanding of the various elements of an organization's financial position to quickly understand the balances and types of assets and liabilities and the composition of net assets. Assets and liabilities are described with the same words in nonprofit and for-profit financial statements. Assets include cash and cash equivalents, accounts receivable, grants receivable, prepaid expenses, property and equipment net of accumulated depreciation, and other assets. Liabilities include accounts payable, accrued expenses, deferred revenue, short- and long-term debt, and other liabilities. A few unique terms may appear in a nonprofit financial statement, such as refundable advances, which are payments received to support activities for which the earning process is not complete.

The primary difference between a Statement of Financial Position and a Balance Sheet is the language used to describe the difference between assets and liabilities.

- Nonprofit: Assets minus Liabilities equals Net Assets
- Commercial: Assets minus Liabilities equals Equity

There are two classes of net assets – net assets with donor restriction and net assets without donor restriction. They collectively represent the resources that can be applied to the mission of the organization or have already been invested in property and equipment or could be tied up in receivables, prepaid expenses or other assets.

Contributions with a time or purpose restriction are first carried in net assets with donor restriction until those restrictions are met, at which point they are reclassified to net assets without donor restriction and can be used to cover related expenses. I decided to give my high school a multi-year pledge for the annual fund so that I could plan without needing to weigh a decision each year, and they could save a phone call or letter. This is an example of a gift with a time restriction since the gift is intended to support several future periods and will be funded in those periods. An event sponsorship for an event scheduled the following year would also suggest a time restriction. Funding for a specific program or a capital gift are examples of purpose restrictions. The restrictions are released as and when the program operates or when the capital item is placed in service.

Net assets without donor restriction are those that remain after expenses are deducted from unrestricted revenue or net assets released from restriction. Those with donor restriction can only be used for the purpose or during the time, though they aren't necessarily held in cash, so some of the balance could be offset with a pledge receivable. Net investment in property and equipment is most often supported by net assets without donor restriction, so analysis is required to determine how much of net assets without donor restriction are supported by cash and investments.

On that latter point, it is possible to have positive net assets without restriction that are illiquid—they could be completely offset by the net investment in property equipment, receivables or other assets and any cash balances may be attributable to outstanding accounts payable, deferred revenue, or restricted gifts. This signals a caution for readers of nonprofit financial statements—some parties mistakenly refer to net assets without restriction as *reserves*, but in fact only a portion of them, if any, may be liquid and can be drawn down in the event of shortfalls or hardships. This has tripped up many of my clients and board colleagues over the years and required some adjustment in expectations once liquidity is better understood.

I created an example below to analyze the composition of net assets to determine how much true liquidity is available to make reasoned judgments about investments or taking on risks. Of the $1.9 million in net assets without restriction,

$750,000 are invested in property and equipment, another $500,000 is still outstanding as an account receivable, leaving only about $500,000 held in cash.

Line Item	Total	Restricted	Debt/Other	Unrestricted
Cash and cash equivalents	$1,500,000	$ 500,000	$ 500,000	$ 500,000
Accounts or contributions receivable	3,000,000	2,000,000	450,000	550,000
Prepaid expenses and other assets	600,000			600,000
Property and equipment, net	1,000,000		250,000	750,000
Total Assets	$6,100,000	$2,500,000	$1,200,000	$2,400,000
Accounts payable and accrued exp	$ 950,000		950,000	
Deferred revenue	500,000			500,000
Debt	250,000		250,000	
Total Liabilities	$1,700,000		$1,200,000	$ 500,000
Net assets without donor restriction	$1,900,000			$1,900,000
Net assets with donor restriction	2,500,000	2,500,000		
Total Net Assets	$4,400,000	$2,500,000	$1,200,000	$2,400,000
Total Liabilities and Net Assets	$6,100,000	$2,500,000	$1,200,000	$2,400,000

The balance of the analysis for this example reflects that $2 million of the $2.5 million of net assets with restriction have not yet been collected, $250,000 of debt was incurred to purchase property and equipment, and $450,000 of the outstanding vendor liabilities are offset by amounts due from funders.

Nonprofit organizations will frequently use board designations to establish reserves from within net assets without donor restriction, but it is important to ensure those reserves are supported by cash or investments that can be leveraged to fund the specified purpose. When such a designation is made, the financial statements or notes will show two or more categories of net assets without restriction—board designated net assets in one or more categories and undesignated net assets without donor restriction.

Statement of Activities

This statement provides information on the key types of revenue and support, as well as the categories of expenses, grouped into those activities that impact net assets without donor restriction separate from those activities that impact net assets with donor restriction. While many people focus largely on the total column that nets the columns for net assets with and without donor restriction, I encourage financial statement readers to appreciate the usefulness of the information in the separate columns.

Net assets with donor restriction only represent those contributions, grants or earnings that are restricted to a future time or purpose. When a purpose or time restriction is met, the net assets are released from restriction and reclassified to net assets without donor restriction to cover expenses, all of which are reported as changes to net assets without donor restriction. I often describe the changes in net assets without donor restriction as most closely aligned with the results of current operations, excluding only those resources that were given for work not yet performed or for a future period. It is extremely useful, however, to also see gifts, contributions and earnings that are restricted for a future period or purpose because they represent resources that either directly, or through the earnings they generate, will supplement resources to be raised in those future periods.

	Without Donor Restriction	With Donor Restriction	Total
Revenue and Support			
Program services fees	$15,000,000		$15,000,000
Contributions and grants	7,500,000	4,000,000	11,500,000
Investment income	750,000		750,000
Net assets released from restriction	1,500,000	(1,500,000)	
Total Revenue	$24,750,000	$2,500,000	$27,250,000
Expenses			
Program Services	$21,000,000		$21,000,000
Supporting Services			
Management and general	1,900,000		1,900,000
Fundraising	1,100,000		1,100,000
Total Supporting Services	3,000,000		3,000,000
Total Expenses	$24,000,000		$24,000,000
Change in Net Assets	750,000	2,500,000	3,250,000
Net Assets, Opening	12,000,000	1,800,000	13,800,000
Net Assets, Ending	$12,750,000	$4,300,000	$17,050,000

This presentation follows FASB guidance for financial reporting for nonprofit organizations. There is some variation of presentation for nonprofits that have for-profit consolidated subsidiaries or are in categories such as hospitals that need to present information in accordance with other reporting standards as well. Some organizations may strike a subtotal after expenses for a measure of operating performance, and then non-operating items are shown below that. Such items include endowment or capital gifts, gains or losses on the sales of fixed assets, changes in the value of marketable securities, changes in the value of third-party trusts, and non-operating changes related to the liability for post-employment benefits. Reporting these separately enables a better understanding of the results of operations that might otherwise be clouded by non-operating items.

A positive change in net assets with donor restriction in the middle column indicates the organization generated additional resources in support of future activities, and a negative change in net asset with donor restriction indicates the organization is carrying less resources dedicated to future activities than it brought into the current year. In the liquidity analysis in the section above, net assets with donor restriction may not be held in cash, but instead may still be outstanding as a receivable and require follow-up to ensure collection. It is important to understand how much an organization has on hand for future periods and how much may be at risk should collection activities fail.

Statement of Cash Flows

The statement of cash flows is designed to show the sources and uses of cash, broken into three categories—cash flow from operating activities, cash flow from investing activities, and cash flow from financing activities.

- Cash flows from operating activities are receipts from grants, contributions, program service fees, and other sources and disbursements for operating costs such as grants, personnel, professional services, occupancy, supplies, and other such expenses.
- Cash flows from investing activities include the purchase of long-lived assets or marketable securities, or the proceeds from the sale of them, as well as loans made and collected.
- Cash flows from financing activities include both proceeds from or repayments of debt, as well as gifts for capital purposes or endowment. Debt includes working capital lines of credit, equipment financing, mortgages, or bonds.

The statement can be prepared using a direct or an indirect method. The statement starts with the change in total net assets, which is essentially the difference between operating and nonoperating revenues and expenses on an accrual basis. Since both revenue and expenses are recognized in the statement of activities when earned or incurred rather than when they are collected or paid, the statement of cash flows is designed to the activities and changes in balances that impact cash. There are also supplemental disclosures reported at the bottom of the statement of cash flows for interest paid and accrued, as well as non-cash investing and financing activities.

Schedule (or Statement) of Functional Expenses

The reporting standard applicable to nonprofit organizations requires that they provide information about both the function and natural classification of expenses. This presentation of the expense information provides readers with a rich source of information as to how resources are deployed against the work of the organization. This is accomplished by allocating expenses to specific programs and supporting services based on their primary purpose or benefit to the organization. The presentation in this statement shows a column for each major program area as well as a total for all programs, followed by columns for supporting services, which include both management and general costs and fundraising costs.

- *Program Services Expenses*: These are expenses directly related to the NFP's core mission or purpose. For example, if a charity's mission is to provide educational services, expenses related to teaching materials, instructors' salaries, and program administration would be classified as program services expenses.

- **Management and General Expenses:** These are expenses that support the overall operation of the organization, but are not directly tied to program delivery. Examples include general administration expenses like office rent, utilities, and administrative staff salaries.

- **Fundraising Expenses:** These are expenses incurred in the process of soliciting contributions and other forms of financial support. This includes costs related to fundraising events, donor outreach, and marketing campaigns.

There are rows for each major natural class of expense, including grants made, salaries, fringe benefits, professional services, occupancy, depreciation and interest. From this schedule, one can see how personnel or other costs are distributed across the various activities, the overall spending for fundraising relative to other expenses, and how management and general expenses relate to program and fundraising costs.

Program-Specific Reporting

Some funding sources may require financial reports on their funded activities, along with any cost share or matching support. These are usually prescribed in the funding documents and generally tracked with the top categories of personnel, equipment, supplies, travel, contractual, other direct costs, and allocated indirect costs. These are usually presented on a full accrual basis to match expenses to the relevant performance period under the agreement. It is important to ensure all expenses intended to be recovered from a specific funder have been incurred during the performance period, unless an extension has been granted by the funder that would allow final closeout costs to be incurred after the original award period.

It is important to note instances in which the performance period for a funded program does not start or end within the fiscal year. In this case, the award will span more than one fiscal year and may end at a point during the fiscal year when closing procedures may not be as robust as the year-end close. The interim closing date requires additional attention to program expense accruals at the end of the grant period. To ensure the reporting picks up expenses in both the year in which the award started and the year in which it ends, there is a separate reporting approach of a *grant life report*. Fortunately, many accounting software packages will support a grant period separate from the fiscal year, but the reports will need to be set up carefully with the standalone program budget entered over the staggered period as well.

Internal Financial Reports

As explained at the start of the chapter, most internal users of financial information need to primarily understand performance against the budget at a departmental or organizational level and for individual funding sources. Internal users also need information on asset, liability, and net asset balances throughout the year to monitor liquidity, collections, and trends in financial metrics that may trigger compliance problems. Boards of some organizations may use reporting largely similar to that used by management, perhaps at a less granular level, such as by division rather than individual programs. Other boards may receive financial reports closer in format to year-end external financial statements. Boards should work closely with the chief executive and management to understand the dynamics unique to the organization and negotiate a balance of effort against the usefulness of data.

Much attention is paid in interim financial reporting to spending against budgets. Thankfully, that is often the easiest to report. Many expense transactions are fairly straightforward and flow through the accounting processes smoothly, get posted to ledgers, and reflect in financial statements without needing additional effort beyond capturing accruals for expenses that haven't been fully approved and posted. Reporting of actual versus budgeted expenses is usually reported at a cost center level as well as rolled up by department, division, function, and organization wide. These reports help management adjust spending and expectations throughout the year.

Those organizations with primarily transactional revenue streams such as admissions, patient fees and dues are more easily able to close and report on revenue each month than those with service delivery drawn out over time or grants and contracts that require more detailed calculations based on actual expenses. Revenue recognition rules may require an analysis of contracts against criteria for contracts with customers to determine the basis and against what activities revenue must be recognized. Other agreements may need to be reviewed to determine whether a contribution or gift is conditional and, if so, how it will be determined when conditions are met. Contributions can also be either restricted or unrestricted. Those with time or purpose restrictions will flow into net assets with donor restriction, are reported in a separate category in the financial statements and only reclassified to net assets without donor restriction as restrictions are met. Some revenue may be tentative because the earning process is not complete. When a student enrolls for a new semester, for example, they have initiated a transaction from which they can withdraw within a few weeks during the add/drop period.

Accountants generally have a basis for using estimates to record revenue, but management and the board should understand they may not know with precision the amount of ultimate revenue, and should be cognizant of that when interpreting results. Year-end financial reporting usually allows sufficient time for extra analysis or calculations and, depending on the way the business cycle falls within the fiscal year, may have a cleaner cut-off for the earning process for a significant percentage of revenue for the year.

Management and boards should also review statements of financial position regularly to monitor cash balances, collections, potentially growing liabilities, and overall net asset balances. As discussed in greater detail in the chapter on resource management, nonprofits that carry debt are then subject to debt covenants, and compliance with those covenants needs to be reported at least annually but at times on an interim basis as well. If key financial metrics that will impact access to credit or the cost of credit show warning signs, leadership needs to get ahead of those trends where possible to mitigate an otherwise negative impact.

Key Points about Financial Statements

Financial position and the results of activities are critical measures of performance and capacity for future performance. Internal and external financial statements and reports are often complex in their presentation and not fully understood. It is essential that all board members, chief executives, and management teams understand how to read them and use the information they provide in making critical decisions in their work.

- Financial reporting is one of the most important tools the board and management have to monitor financial performance, and management's inability to produce timely reporting can undermine the ability of the board and chief executive to have meaningful discussions of performance and risk.

- At the end of each year, gifts that were received restricted for a future time or unfulfilled purpose will be carried forward as net assets with donor restrictions. During the year, some of the restrictions may be met and then reported as unrestricted.

- Unearned revenues—meaning conditional cash or pledges, or advances for goods yet to be delivered or services yet to be performed—will not be recognized as revenue in any net asset category and instead will be carried as a liability on the Statement of Financial Position.

Strengthen Compliance and Risk Management Practices

Management is responsible while boards are accountable for ensuring an organization complies with government laws, regulations and grant or contractual requirements. This is an instance in which the complementary roles of the board and management are particularly clear. It is the board's role to ensure management has appropriate processes and controls in place to monitor and fulfill these requirements. This is accomplished through a system of internal control—processes, policies and procedures designed to ensure an organization achieves its objectives and compliance. This section of the book provides both the board and management with an understanding of the context for and significance of having strong compliance and risk management practices.

Failure to comply with tax filing, licensure renewal or other filing requirements are usually met with fines until compliance is achieved. Initial failure to comply with internal control, financial reporting, regulatory or other standards often results in required remediation on the part of the organization through the filing of a plan of correction prior to fines being imposed. As a practical matter, governments need nonprofit organizations to deliver critical programs and resources to communities, so it is more advantageous to help an organization get back on track if it strays than to risk a gap in service to vulnerable populations. Some government agencies even offer training and technical assistance to nonprofit organizations to assist them in learning and implementing best practices to attain compliance. To the extent appropriate remediation isn't accomplished, sanctions can become increasingly punitive, including significant fines and loss of financial support, withholding licenses, and ultimately forcing closure, but only after efforts to achieve compliance have failed.

Nonprofit boards are increasingly focused on compliance and risk management because of the heightened awareness of these matters following the passage of the Sarbanes-Oxley Act of 2002 (SOX), enacted in response to commercial accounting scandals in the late 1990s and early 2000s. The goal of the SOX legislation was to increase transparency and thereby strengthen the internal control environments of public companies. SOX accomplished this through expanded disclosure and audit requirements, and to that end established the Public Company Accounting Oversight Board.

The reason this is in a book focused on the nonprofit sector is that in addition to the best practices emerging from this legislation, there are provisions that apply to all entities as well as others that apply to nonprofits with publicly traded debt securities. This heightened focus on compliance and risk management requires strong collaboration between boards and management to ensure the efforts drive the organization to optimize the way it operates within a strong control environment.

The role of the board is performed by the committee charged with oversight of compliance and risk management, sometimes as part of an audit committee charter. The oversight of compliance and risk management practices mandated by SOX and encouraged by the resulting best practice requires regular communication from management to the board, along with the board's active engagement with the information provided. Reporting on the functioning of internal controls and any mitigating actions required to address gaps or control failures is designed to drive transparency and accountability with the expectation that the check and balance will result in stronger control environments through active remediation of any gaps or shortfall observed.

I have served both on an Audit, Risk and Compliance committee of a board of directors and as a consultant assisting management in reporting to one. Management and boards each have distinct and complementary roles in the areas of compliance and risk management. Boards have ultimate accountability for compliance, so in their monitoring and oversight they should ensure the executive has dedicated sufficient resources to monitor and remediate compliance and risk management issues. They can accomplish this by receiving regular reporting on monitoring and remediation activities, inquiring of management about the controls in place in key areas and how management is monitoring them, as well as when and how management remediates compliance or control failures.

This is where the relationship between management and the board needs to be strong. Given the pace of change in organizations, controls need to be regularly reviewed to ensure they are updated as systems, work processes, and organizational roles change. With staff and leadership changes across multiple functions, it is not surprising that controls may break down or not operate as intended. Board effectiveness is enhanced when the board includes members with relevant professional experience. If a board does not have relevant experience in key areas, they should engage with experts to provide education and guidance so they can effectively oversee compliance and risk. Fortunately, the nonprofit sector has a wealth of resources available to inform us about various requirements. The board should, at a minimum, avail themselves of these resources.

Enterprise Risk Management (ERM)

The Committee of Sponsoring Organizations of the Treadway Commission (COSO) launched an integrated framework for risk management in 1992. At this point in its evolution, the COSO framework was presented as a pyramid, with the internal control environment as its foundation. There were three actions—risk assessment, control activities, and monitoring—within an overall environment of regular and sustained information and communication. At its core, the framework requires an entity to complete a risk assessment, document the control environment, monitor its performance and functioning, and then remediate any gaps or breakdowns observed. At the same time, ERM as a practice and strategy was gaining traction in many organizations, with an increasing focus on board oversight of risk management. Beyond just the COSO approach, ERM is the broadest view of risk looking across an organization and encompasses financial, operational, strategic, and legal risks. It is a framework for risk management that is designed to:

61

- Identify and assess risks
- Prioritize risks, focusing on the greatest exposures
- Develop and integrate mitigation strategies into business processes
- Monitor and report on their effectiveness
- Update and adjust strategies as needed to drive continuous improvement

With the passage of SOX, there has been a renewed interest in the COSO framework as a path to comply with the new law. In 2013, COSO made significant enhancements to the framework by establishing seven principles across five categories—the control environment, the risk assessment process, control activities, information and communication, and monitoring activities. The enhanced framework continues to serve well as a foundation for risk management. There are five steps to adoption:

1. Develop awareness, expertise and alignment
2. Conduct a preliminary impact assessment
3. Facilitate broad awareness, training and comprehensive assessment
4. Develop and execute the COSO transition plan
5. Drive continuous improvement

This is the responsibility of management; it should be sufficiently resourced and made a visible management priority. Boards should factor in risk as an integral part of organizational strategy. Again, the board's role is to ensure there are adequate systems and controls in place, and that they are being monitored through regular reporting from management or an in-house or contracted internal audit function. The board needs to weigh risks and the cost to mitigate various risks in balancing the resources allocated to control risks versus other organizational activities.

Internal Audit and Monitoring Controls

The board and management share responsibility for creating the culture and "tone at the top" needed to promote an environment with strong ethical standards, internal controls, oversight mechanisms, and diligence across the enterprise. An audit or other committee of the board may have responsibility for oversight of risk management, including receiving reports directly from an internal audit function to ensure management is monitoring the effectiveness of the control environment and acting to address any identified issues. For the board to provide effective oversight of risk and compliance, management needs to have robust documentation of risks and compliance requirements, the internal controls designed to mitigate risk, and activities to monitor the operation of those controls.

Internal controls have long been an element of a strong and robust accounting, financial reporting, and compliance environment. We can take a hint of the importance of these areas by looking at the audit requirements placed on organizational recipients of federal awards, which require auditors to test and report on internal control over financial reporting and compliance. My experience with smaller, less complex organizations that are new to federal awards is that they struggle to design and implement controls that didn't seem necessary before. Fortunately, OMB's Uniform Guidance clearly articulates the requirements, and many nonprofits make their policies available online, so there is a lot of material available from which to draw. This freely available material can be a guide, but organizations should think about how similar controls should be implemented and operate in their environment. I have worked with several organizations that realized they needed to upgrade their controls and related documentation and helped them design and document compliant controls appropriate to their work.

Because accounting is the accumulation of possibly hundreds of thousands—if not millions—of individual transactions, internal controls are critical in ensuring that transactions are properly authorized, accurately recorded, and reported in accordance with U.S. GAAP. There are two key events that internal controls are generally designed to detect or prevent— either errors or malicious acts such as fraud. Given that people outside the accounting function initiate transactions and need to provide information on their purpose and thus how they should be charged, errors in accounting may not always be made by accounting personnel but instead those originating a transaction. Internal controls are designed to have layers of review and verification of the substance of and accounting for a transaction before it is completed.

There are many other areas where internal controls are critical in preventing or detecting fraud, reckless errors, and theft. Errors or fraud can occur and go undetected when controls break down or don't operate as intended. Under SOX, public companies and nonprofit organizations that have issued publicly traded debt instruments are required to document and test their controls, and their external auditors are required to review the monitoring program and report on its effectiveness as part of the annual audit. While SOX speaks mostly to issuers of publicly traded debt and securities, specific provisions of the law apply to all entities, not just public companies—whistleblower protections and criminal penalties for destruction, alteration, or falsification of documents with the intent to impede investigations. All nonprofits should be aware of these requirements, and boards should ensure management has mechanisms in place to comply.

Internal controls are only effective if they are clearly documented so that the required review step is clear and can be monitored. In developing policies and procedures in accounting and other areas, controls should be designed to address risks inherent in the process. For example, if there is a risk that an employee would incorrectly report their hours on a timesheet, having a timesheet reviewed and approved by a supervisor with knowledge of the employee's work may serve as an effective control. This control is explicitly identified in OMB's Uniform Guidance as a requirement for federal award recipients who charge labor to federal awards. Once documented, the controls can be monitored and tested.

It is demoralizing for management and frustrating for boards to be surprised by errors that aren't caught because of gaps in controls or poorly operating controls. Control breakdown surprises drive a wedge between the board and management since they are key components in a well-managed environment, and it causes boards to lose confidence. Surprises include billing errors that may result in claw-backs from funding sources, corrections to previously issued financial statements because of accounting errors, or losses from fraud. Documenting controls helps management evaluate whether there are gaps to be filled, as well as enable the controls to be monitored and tested. These best practices help organizations quickly identify and respond to issues as they arise, which helps build the board's confidence in management and strengthen alignment.

Not every nonprofit organization can rationalize the cost of an internal audit function but, as part of an overall risk assessment, consideration should be given whether such a function might be justified based on the nature of the risks. Regardless of size or scale, organizations do not need to stand up an in-house internal audit function to avail themselves of this capacity. Most accounting firms and some other consulting firms offer internal audit services. Because of the independence required to perform external financial statement audits, the same firm cannot perform both the annual financial statement audit and an internal audit function.

External auditors evaluate the control environment (1) because their professional standards require them to do so in determining how to design audit procedures and (2) in the context of a single audit that requires auditors to test and report on internal control over financial reporting and internal control over compliance. An internal audit plan starts with an identification and ranking of the various risks an organization faces—including financial, legal, compliance, and reputational risk—as well as the detective and preventive controls in place in each major business process. The resulting risk register helps the organization focus on testing the most significant areas of risk, and internal audit plans will cycle through most major business processes over two to three years.

One of the most powerful examples of respectful collaboration I've seen is while serving on the Audit, Risk and Compliance committee for Children's National Hospital. The organization hears regularly from both the external financial statement auditors and an outsourced internal audit function. There is a robust internal audit program guided by a plan that prioritizes risks and incorporates follow-up to ensure corrective actions have been taken and are effective. This committee perhaps more than any other highlights the respective roles of management and the board. The presentations to and discussions with the committee elevate the importance of the control environment and follow-through on remediation.

Fraud Risk

Nonprofit organizations are not immune from fraud, and indeed may be more vulnerable as they attempt to do important work with limited resources. Extreme cases such as the falsification of records, misappropriation of funds and embezzlement can expose the organization to increased public scrutiny, result in the loss of funding relationships, and deplete critical resources. Fraud often starts small, as perpetrators test the boundaries of what is possible. Preventive controls stop a perpetrator from successfully executing a fraud, but if a fraudulent act succeeds, it's important to have controls in place to detect fraud should it occur and quickly remediate the issues to limit potential financial losses. Many of the most publicly reported examples were the result of fraud going unchecked for extended periods until its brazenness made it impossible to ignore.

In the 1990s, the United Way of America (UWA) suffered a significant loss of support and donor confidence following discovery of fraudulent acts by its to that point lauded CEO, which upon investigation spanned at least a decade. There were numerous gaps in internal controls and a lax attitude on the part of the board toward oversight of executive spending and internal controls. A later CEO reflected on that period, writing in the Harvard Business Review:

"United Way [of America] suffered a scandal involving the longtime CEO, who was convicted in 1995 of fraud and conspiracy and sentenced to federal prison. Much of the decade was spent recovering from that by revamping our governance and operations, writing a new code of ethics, and tightening up our brand management."[5]

We know from court filings that some of the conduct included complicit employees who mischaracterized expenses they processed for reimbursement on behalf of the CEO. Because of the corporate structure, there was no one on staff to review and approve the CEO's expenses. As part of its oversight role, the board should review—at least periodically—credit card charges or reimbursements to the chief executive to flag any questionable excessive spending.

What is also problematic in this case is that even as the board was becoming aware of the fraud in early 1992, the Executive Committee gave the CEO a vote of confidence twice and rejected his resignation. The CEO would later use those facts in his pursuit of deferred benefits to say that since these votes occurred after the board was aware of the fraud, they forfeited their right to terminate him or recover damages for the conduct. Fortunately for United Way, the judge in the case determined that the board only had awareness of some

---

[5] United Way's CEO on Shifting a Century-Old Business Model, Brian Gallagher, Harvard Business Review, September-October 2018

impropriety but not the full depth and breadth of it and found that the board had not forfeited its rights.[6] The board would have served the organization better by simply withholding judgment and comment until they had more information. The scandal had a significant impact on fundraising for a few years, and the organization had to rebuild trust with its donors.

In one organization, I discovered the staff person responsible for payroll processing had overpaid themselves by recording hours in a different cost center so that the time charges in the accounting department looked normal. They went to great lengths to conceal the theft—they blocked out the portion of the printed payroll register that included their charges in the other department, so a visual review of the report wouldn't have revealed the additional payment. While there should certainly have been better preventive controls in place, there were detective controls through the monthly budget vs. actual reporting. We saw labor in one cost center that was higher than anticipated, and we worked our way back through the details in the reports. We manually added the totals on the printed reports and discovered that something was missing. Working with the payroll service, we were able to identify the fraudulent hours.

Fraud can also come from outside the organization; thus controls should be in place to prevent or detect it. Some criminals will create checks with an organization's banking information and try to get them cashed. Most banks have a

---

[6]   Final order in Aramony v. United Way of America, 28 F. Supp. 2d 147 (S.D.N.Y. 1998)
       https://law.justia.com/cases/federal/district-courts/FSupp2/28/147/2531777/

"positive pay" program that will only clear checks that have been uploaded by the bank customer before being presented, and the bank will note when they clear, so someone trying to present a second copy of a check will also be unsuccessful. Another example of fraud from outside the organization is the submission of a false claim for benefits or other payments. Controls should be developed to verify claims through additional documentation supporting eligibility and verifying whether already eligible recipients previously submitted the same claim.

Insurance

Risk management also entails the appropriate use of insurance to guard against insurable events such as casualty, theft, employment practices, errors and omissions, and cyber threats. Oversight of the insurance program should also be within the remit of the committee responsible for oversight of risk management. The board's role here is to ensure the types of coverage and coverage limits are sufficiently comprehensive and robust to protect against the financial impact of insurable risks. Organizations providing various types of health and human services will have different exposures because of the potential harm to service recipients. Malpractice and/or professional liability coverage is critical in these settings. The higher education sector has a similar category of coverage termed educators' liability.

Standard coverages that almost all organizations should carry include:

- General liability

- Automobile liability
- Property and casualty
- Employment practices liability
- Fiduciary liability for retirement plans
- Directors' and officers' liability

Cyber insurance is an increasingly important coverage type for organizations with risk of liability in the event of a data breach. Some organizations still haven't started carrying this type of insurance. Early on, the primary risk had been the loss or disclosure of sensitive data such as health data or personal financial data such as social security or credit card numbers. Ransomware attacks are a newer and growing risk that begin with criminals locking access to critical business data and functionality and demanding ransom to restore access. The impact of such an attack may prevent an organization from conducting day-to-day business, from billing and transactional systems to safety systems. An attack could result in the loss of critical business data in addition to interrupting operations. Not all cyber policies will cover this risk, so organizations should clearly understand covered risks and exclusions.

Board members come from diverse backgrounds that provide additional perspective to the appropriate use of insurance. I worked with one organization that had an insurance broker on the board who was extremely helpful in educating both the board and management on insurable risks, guided them through the selection of a qualified third-party broker, and gave guidance on coverage limits, claims experience and other important elements in selecting insurance providers.

Disaster Recovery/Business Continuity Planning

While some nonprofits are involved in disaster response, the concept of disaster recovery relates to when an organization faces a disaster that may impact its ability to continue operating on a day-to-day basis. There are a number of disasters that can impact a nonprofit organization, from natural disasters that impact the organization's ability to access facilities or data and thus perform its day-to-day work to purely technology-driven disasters that impact access to data. Increased cyber threats threaten many organizations in ways not previously contemplated, when the issue was a data center going down because one part of the country was impacted by a natural disaster. Ransomware attacks are an increasing reality for commercial and nonprofit organizations alike, any of which can be targeted and risk losing access to critical data.

Business continuity focuses on the ability to ramp up operations from an alternate location, as well as being able to cut over to redundant data centers to continue critical operations when a primary data location is compromised. Boards should work with management to ensure plans are in place to respond to a broad range of threats, leveraging redundant data centers and alternative bases of operations to continue an organization's critical work serving its community. For those providing health or other critical human services, such a plan may include safely transitioning vulnerable people to a safe environment from which to continue receiving services.

Federal and State Tax Compliance

Compliance with Federal tax filing requirements applies to all nonprofit organizations, regardless of whether they receive government funding or are otherwise subject to government compliance requirements. All the approximately 2 million nonprofits registered with the IRS must comply with annual filing requirements—approximately 115,000 private foundations file Form 990-PF and another almost 500,000 nonprofit organizations with gross receipts greater than $50,000 file Form 990 or 990-EZ.[7] As noted earlier, churches are not required to file Form 990, even though some church-related organizations that are exempt from filing do so for transparency to donors. Any active nonprofit that isn't required to file Form 990, 990-EZ or 990-PF is required to file Form 990-N, also known as the e-postcard, since it must be filed electronically. All filings are due by the 15th of the 5th month after the close of the fiscal year and can be extended up to six months. Any returns not filed on time (by the 15th of the 5th month or the 15th of the 11th month if properly extended) are subject to late filing penalties. Organizations with gross receipts less than $1,208,500 (effective in 2024, adjusted annually) are subject to a $20 per day penalty up to $12,000, and all other organizations are subject to a $120 per day penalty up to $60,000 (also effective in 2024 and adjusted annually). Any organization that fails to file any return for three consecutive years will automatically lose their tax-exempt status.

---

[7] https://www.irs.gov/statistics/soi-tax-stats-charities-and-other-tax-exempt-organizations-statistics and https://www.irs.gov/statistics/soi-tax-stats-domestic-private-foundation-and-charitable-trust-statistics

We'll talk about resource generation later, but as management and board members consider alternatives to generate resources, they should be aware of the tax rules surrounding unrelated business income. Some unrelated business activities make financial sense even though they may be subject to tax, but understanding the potential tax impact is important. The key elements in determining whether an activity is unrelated and therefore subject to tax include:

- Whether it is a trade or business
- Whether it is regularly carried on
- If it is not substantially related

There are several explicit exclusions unique to nonprofit settings outlined in the tax law that are *not* considered unrelated:

- Any trade or business conducted with volunteer labor
- Any trade or business carried on for the convenience of members, students, patients, officers or employees
- Any trade or business selling donated merchandise
- Bingo games in jurisdictions where for-profit entities don't regularly carry on bingo games

Nonprofit investments in partnerships are considered a trade or business and almost always subject to unrelated business income tax.

With respect to state and local government compliance, there are also some tax filing requirements as well as registration, licensing, and employment-related responsibilities, amongst others. Thirty-five states require a copy of Form 990 to be filed along with any charitable registrations due. Any organization with unrelated business income that files a Form 990-T will also have to file a state corporate income tax return for that income.

Nonprofit organizations with qualified retirement plans established under IRC Sect. 401(k) or 403(b) are required to file Form 5500 with the U.S. Department of Labor (DOL). Those plans that have more than 100 participants are required to also have audited financial statements for the plans, and those audited statements must be filed along with Form 5500.

Licensing and other Regulation

Many nonprofit organizations perform work in healthcare or human services that are subject to state and local regulation and licensing requirements, which may include standards for facilities, personnel, and planning. Educational institutions with on-campus housing, food service, and health services will need licenses to operate those facilities. In fact, nonprofits aren't much different from commercial operations touching different areas that states regulate for safety reasons. Across the many types of organizations beyond just health and human services, requirements may relate to child welfare, food handling, medication administration, animal control, building codes, professional licensing, and in some cases just a general business license.

Failure to maintain required licenses could expose the organization to sanctions and put it at significant risk of closure, so the board should work with management to develop dashboards or other tracking that will enable the board to monitor conditions, processes, and actions that will have an impact on licensing determinations. Facilities in which services are provided, supplies are stored, or meals are prepared may be inspected for cleanliness, sufficient medication or food, and safety. Regulators will require certification showing whether licensed professionals have met continuing education or experience requirements. Certain policies and procedures may be required—incident management procedures, emergency response and escalation procedures, or disaster recovery plans—along with evidence they are being followed.

Charitable organizations are also subject to a unique subset of state and local laws related to how they raise funds. While charitable solicitation registration, described below, impacts almost all nonprofits, commercial co-ventures are less understood and, in some states, strictly regulated so they are described below as well.

Charitable Solicitation Registration

Most people in nonprofit organizations are unaware of the level of regulation and compliance surrounding fundraising. The development or advancement office usually works closely with the accounting and finance team to complete and submit all the required registrations each year, and a combination of the CEO, CFO and a board treasurer are usually required to sign them. I've summarized the general requirements below.

States' Attorneys General are usually tasked with representing the public interest with respect to nonprofit organizations, often requiring any charity that will solicit donations in their state to file an initial registration and then annual or biannual filings. These registrations are used to report information about funds raised, types of solicitations, whether paid fundraisers are used, and the current executives and board members. They also may require copies of Forms 990 as attachments. As of this writing, only eight states require neither charitable registrations nor disclosure statements. Direct mail into a state generally triggers registration, subject to some minimum thresholds in some states, and raising money online also generally exposes an organization to registration requirements across most states that require it. Fortunately, there are several companies that provide registration support and coordination, which may make sense to ensure there are no compliance problems down the line.

Almost all states regulate charitable games—bingo, raffles, and other games of chance—including those with no other charitable registration requirements. Not surprisingly, these are often regulated by the state agency that operates the state lottery. While games of chance may not be used widely, those organizations who use them should be aware of the requirements, which can be confirmed by checking your state's website.

Commercial Co-Ventures

For-profit entities with a consumer customer base represent an opportunity for nonprofits to generate support in collaboration with such a business. Such a co-venture links a donation to a consumer purchase, hence the commercial aspect to the activity. The donation can take several forms—as a percentage of the sale, a fixed amount tied to a specific purchase, or a round-up at the point of purchase. From a charity's standpoint, whether required by law in the states in which it operates, the charity should always try to document the understanding between the parties. I'd suggest looking to the requirements in states that do regulate commercial co-ventures:

- Define the time period for the promotion
- Identify fees that may be deducted from the donation prior to disbursement
- Describe when and in what form donations will be distributed and what type of accounting will be provided to the charity
- Ensure the charity can approve any language describing the charity to be used in the promotion
- Clarify whether the charity will have access to customer information in order to thank customers
- If more than one charity is involved, clear guidelines for how funds will be allocated across the charities

Some organizations have generated a substantial portion of their donations through these co-ventures, often extending their reach for potential donors significantly. The commercial entity benefits by association with the charity, the perception that they are supporting things that are important to their customers, and sometimes even generating press attention.

I worked with an organization that received several million dollars annually from a commercial co-venture along with several other benefiting charities. Per the guidelines above, the manner of allocation was clearly defined in the agreement along with the other required elements. While the organization was headquartered in Washington, DC, the co-venture was with a New York based company, so a copy of the agreement had to be filed with the State of New York.

As of this writing, the District of Columbia does not regulate commercial co-ventures.

Other Compliance Matters

Organizations that receive federal awards, either directly from a federal agency or passed through a non-federal entity such as another nonprofit prime grantee or a state or local government, must comply with the provisions of the OMB's *Uniform Administrative Requirements, Cost Principles, and Audit Requirements for Federal Awards* (Uniform Guidance). Collectively, these specify required system capabilities, documents that must be collected and maintained, policies and procedures that must be in place, how costs are recorded and allocated, and the audit standards that will apply. For those meeting the threshold requiring a single audit, compliance with these provisions, as well as provisions contained within grant agreements, are evaluated and reported on by external auditors. Any findings that rise to the level of a significant deficiency or material weakness must be disclosed by the auditor, and management is required to provide both a response to the underlying finding and a plan of correction that is included in and filed with the single audit report.

Key Points on Compliance and Risk Management

This is an area in which the board and management have distinct but complementary and interactive roles. Accordingly, alignment is critical for each of them to effectively discharge their responsibilities. Similar to my point in the fraud discussion, if the board and management don't have a shared understanding of compliance and risk management practices and work collaboratively to fulfill their respective roles, it is likely there will be more discord than alignment between them.

- The board is accountable to stakeholders for ensuring the organization complies with all laws, regulations, and provisions of any funding agreements and that there are adequate controls and safeguards in place to protect the assets, personnel, and recipients of services.

- Management is responsible for designing and implementing appropriate controls and business processes to ensure compliance and monitoring the effectiveness of controls that protect the assets, personnel and recipients of services.

- Management is also therefore responsible for monitoring the environment and reporting on its monitoring activities and findings. Some organizations may contract with an outside firm to perform an internal control function and may stand one up internally.

Develop a Diversified Resource Generation Strategy

As discussed in the chapter about the many types of nonprofit organizations, there are a variety of ways for nonprofits to generate support and revenue. This chapter will equip boards and management teams with information about the different types of resources that their organizations may pursue and a framework for them to evaluate opportunities and diversify revenue sources. Some alternatives may require significant investment, while others may leverage existing capacity. Any dialogue about revenue sources should ultimately fold into the strategic and annual planning processes.

The nonprofit sector receives revenue and support from a broad range of sources—from federal awards, government and private sector contracts and program service fees, to contributions and grants from philanthropic sources. While many organizations have primary sources of funding driving the bulk of support and revenue, diversification provides greater flexibility to nonprofits, guarding against instability in the primary sources. Most nonprofits are dependent at some level on philanthropy, but they may also receive program-specific grants and contracts, program services fees, membership dues, licensing fees, and proceeds from the sale of goods and services.

Organizations dependent on contributions and grants could explore earned revenue opportunities, while those dependent on program service fees could evaluate the level of investment needed to drive greater philanthropic support. Just like commercial enterprises, organizations need to invest resources in driving revenue, such as a development or advancement function, outreach for organizations serving specific populations, or enrollment for educational institutions. Boards with members from diverse backgrounds can help link the organization with private sector and government contacts who can assist the organization with which they are associated.

I worked with an organization that received an annual federal operating grant for decades. Though there was seemingly no immediate pressure to build other channels of support, they began building relationships with several corporate sponsors in the late 1990s and continued to cultivate and grow that base of support. The organization lost the federal grant in 2011. Were it not for the corporate relationships, the organization would have struggled to continue at all. While they had to adjust to a new spending level and build their way back up, it's a poignant example of how critical it is to have diversified revenue streams. Had the loss of funding been less severe, losing only a portion of the prior grant for example, they would have been well positioned to navigate the fluctuations. They continued to develop those as well as new corporate relationships, and leveraged a new digital strategy to add another potential revenue stream.

In addition to unrestricted fundraising support, many nonprofits generate program service fees, which include tuition, room and board charged by higher education institutions; patient service fees charged by healthcare providers; admission fees charged by museums and cultural institutions; subscription revenue; and membership dues. Government grants are another significant source of restricted support that require a specialized skill in preparing applications for awards and more structured accounting requirements.

Philanthropic Support

Over the past twenty-five years, I've heard countless times from new board members, managers, and staff that the organization with which they are associated should "just fundraise more." To be sure, most nonprofit organizations rely on some level of philanthropic support, but they each have unique constituencies and communities from which to draw that support. Not surprisingly, those with a broader mission that might touch people of all socio-economic backgrounds, or those who serve a wealthier base of individuals altogether, are able to more easily access numerous and large gifts. Organizations serving those in poverty, or a particular subset of them, struggle to raise funds from within the constituency they serve and are more dependent on the "kindness of strangers." It's important to determine what role philanthropy can play in an organization's revenue mix and at what level.

When I took the reins of the developmental disability services provider, we were heavily dependent on government funding. Sources included Medicaid funding for intermediate care facilities and home and community-based services, locally funded human care agreements, daily rates from the public school system and office of early childhood development, and federal funding for a series of research and demonstration projects. We had great volunteer and modest financial support from the local Knights of Columbus chapters but also a limited base of donors overall. As one of several social concerns agencies serving the local Catholic community, we made a concerted effort to build our donor base but were competing with other agencies for resources from the local Catholic community. We continued to develop support from some families served and other constituencies, but a need to simplify messaging to the Catholic community was ultimately one of the reasons the entity was merged into a larger, related organization.

The most significant category of nonprofit organizations—public charities and private foundations exempt from tax under IRC section 501(c)(3)—can attract tax-deductible support. The individual deduction for charitable contributions has been a component of U.S. tax law since its origins in the early 1900s. Ratification of the 16th Amendment to the U.S. Constitution granted Congress the power to levy an income tax, and the subsequent Revenue Act of 1913 established the modern federal income tax system. The individual tax deduction for charitable contributions originated in the War Revenue Act of 1917. To fund government costs in fighting World War I, tax rates were substantially increased for all income levels, moving the top rate from 15% to 67% for incomes over $2 million. The charitable deduction was created because Congress was concerned the higher taxes would discourage philanthropy. The corporate tax deduction for charitable contributions was enacted in 1936.

Research has generally found that the tax deductibility of charitable contributions positively influences giving, but may also impact the allocation of donations based on how limits apply to deductible amounts. IRC section 501 was established in the Revenue Act of 1954, setting out the different classifications of exempt entities. The Tax Reform Act of 1969 introduced rules related to private inurement and excess benefit transactions to limit the use of tax-exempt organizations for personal gain. These laws created the environment that has enabled the nonprofit sector to flourish over the past several decades.

While private foundations can generally fund their operations and programmatic giving solely with investment return, most organizations—even those with endowments—need to expend resources to generate new revenue and support each year. Nonprofits not only look to board members for direct financial support, but to serve as ambassadors in the community and assist in raising awareness and funding from others. Nonprofits who are dependent on government funding for much of their programming have an inherent challenge in convincing donors to support their work. This is, in part, due to potential donors believing the government should be paying for the work, and thus that their philanthropic support would have more impact elsewhere. This is often true of organizations serving the most vulnerable populations.

Any organization categorized under IRC section 501(c)(3) should consider some level of fundraising activity and investment. The charitable deduction incentivizes people with an interest in certain charitable activities to make donations to them. Many organizations rely on philanthropic support to cover some portion of their budget every year. Many grantors will ask about board giving, and the best positioning is to be able to report that 100% of the board donates to the organization each year. Some boards may have financial requirements at a specific dollar level, while others generally ask board members to give within their means and that the organization be a philanthropic priority for them. At all levels, though, donor relationships need to be cultivated, and sufficient resources allocated to outreach and communications that provide information on the organization's work and how a donor's funds were used to drive impact. Board members can make introductions to new donors, and the organization should be prepared to support the ask and follow-up as appropriate.

Earned Revenue

There are many different types of earned revenue, the largest category of which is program service revenue—from patients, students, members, and visitors, among others. Other broad categories include rental income, net investment income, the sale of goods, and various fees (e.g., registration, parking, adoption, lab or late fees). While there may be opportunities to expand the types of earned revenue an organization generates, boards and management should consider the alignment of any work with the mission, the amount of management time that will be required to stand up and oversee new activities, and whether the activities will expose the organization to unrelated business income tax (UBIT). Some taxable activities may still make sense, but it's one of the factors to consider.

Nonprofit organizations can also engage in social enterprise to generate earned revenues. These may include sales of goods and services produced by the population a nonprofit is established to serve. For example, an organization created to provide job training to a disadvantaged group and the training could take the form of work that produces goods for sale, such as teaching trainees to repair donated cars and selling them. There are examples of food service businesses that employ veterans, individuals with disabilities, or the formerly incarcerated, which generate resources for job training and other supporting services to the workers.

A general rule for pursuing incremental earned revenue, though, is that it at least breaks even on a standalone basis—total revenue reduced by the direct costs incurred to generate the revenue. Nonprofits should, generally, only consider new earned revenue opportunities (not core to fulfillment of the mission) that bolster the bottom line. If there are ways to meet the mission with earned revenue, it may be worthy of subsidy, but that puts pressure on other revenue streams. The issues raised by consideration of new earned revenue opportunities should be fully discussed between the board and management prior to investing significant cost or time in the endeavor.

Federal Awards and Other Government Support

The federal government spends more than $1 trillion annually across a broad range of categories of assistance that drive nonprofit activity.[8] Funds are awarded directly to nonprofit organizations as well as to the states, which then award some

---

[8]   https://www.bdo.com/insights/blogs/nonprofit-standard/navigating-the-terrain-of-the-2024-revised-uniform-guidance#:~:text=Key%20 changes%20include%20simplifying%20compliance,missions%20 rather%20than%20bureaucratic%20navigation.

funds to organizations. Federal assistance supports health, social services, education, housing, and employment programs, among other activities. Some of the programs supported by federal awards, such as Head Start and Temporary Assistance to Needy Families, are embedded in our society and help to combat the impacts of poverty. Medicaid provides leverage to state and local funding that supports health and related services for individuals living in poverty and with certain chronic conditions. Innovative programs are designed and implemented as research and demonstration projects with support from Federal agencies.

Organizations that do not regularly pursue federal awards may be able to advance important aspects of their mission by leveraging federal funds, either as a prime grantee or as a sub-recipient. Federal funds come with a variety of constraints. Programs like *Head Start* require that the organizations receiving funding provide a non-federal share of at least 20% of the total program costs. These are sometimes described as a funding match. It is important to understand that raising matching funds alone is not sufficient to meet these requirements, whether funded with additional external support or through existing non-federal resources, any funds applied to meet a non-federal share requirement must be expended on the federal program (hence the language non-federal share).

OMB's Uniform Guidance provides the guidelines that must be followed by organizations that leverage federal awards, including administrative and system requirements, cost principles, and audit requirements. While there may be an added cost of compliance for an organization receiving federal funds for the first time, the policies and procedures, cost principles, internal control and documentation requirements represent best practices that benefit all programs of an organization. Overall, federal awards represent an opportunity to fund innovation and critical medical or health related services and also extend the reach of services to veterans, people living in poverty, or other disadvantaged groups.

Most federal awards are cost accountable for direct and indirect costs. In some limited instances, a federal award can be structured as a fixed amount award, in which cases reasonably reliable cost data needs to be available to estimate the cost but, after the award is made, payment is based on the accomplishment of specific milestones. If priced well, this award type shares risk between the organization and government. Any shortfall in funding must be covered by the recipient, and any savings would accrue to the benefit of the recipient. Organizations who have never previously negotiated an indirect cost rate with a federal agency are able to use a de minimis rate of 10% (increasing to 15% as of the time of this writing), which means they do not have to fully account for indirect costs charged to federal awards. Generally, in applying for a federal award for the first time, an applicant would need to use the de minimis rate in the proposed budget, whether it will fully cover the allocable direct costs or not. In either the case of a fixed amount award or using the de minimis indirect rate, the organization can spend more or less than they receive in federal funds, so it will be important to understand the organization's cost structure when incorporating federal awards in a resource generation strategy.

Revenue Recognition Constraints

I've grouped resource generation and revenue recognition for a specific reason. While generating resources is vital, there are several factors that will impact when support and revenue can be recognized, how it can be used, and how it will impact the financial statements. For instance, receiving a large endowment gift cannot offset an operating deficit, except to the extent of future distributable earnings on the endowment; any organization with an annual fund should be attentive to sustaining annual fund giving, because it is usually both unconditional and unrestricted so it can support current operations with no further outlay. To earn some types of revenue could require the organization to set up new programs and incur additional expense, so securing funding for a program that is strategically important is useful but finding funding for a program that wasn't in the plan may be problematic. Funding with narrow requirements may draw management time and resources away from an organization's primary work and should be carefully evaluated before being accepted.

Unconditional support is recognized as revenue when either an unconditional promise to give is received or when an unconditional gift is received in the form of cash, securities, or other assets. Non-cash support is recorded at its fair market value at the time it is given; if it is later liquidated, there can be a gain or loss on disposition of the asset. Because the market value of certain securities can fluctuate significantly over time, it is best practice to liquidate stock gifts when received. If the organization has an investment pool and investment adviser, an unliquidated stock gift could be managed within the overall investment pool, but the advisers should consider how it impacts the investment mix from the board-approved investment policy as well as the prudence of carrying the individual investment. It is possible that an unconditional gift may nonetheless be restricted, either in perpetuity in the form of an endowment gift, by purpose in the form of a program-specific gift or grant, or by time in the case of a multi-year or deferred gift.

A contribution or promise to give is considered conditional only when there are both (1) a performance-related barrier to be overcome and (2) either a right of return of assets transferred or a right of release from a promisor's obligation to transfer assets.

Example: A challenge grant that is only paid to the extent of matching funds raised, or even only if a threshold of matching funds is met, would be conditional.

Time and purpose constraints will impact when and how revenue is accounted for and reported in financial statements—which is critical to managing bottom line performance. Boards and management should understand whether the constraints on funding will enable it to offset current costs or be carried to a future period as either deferred revenue or net assets with donor restriction. Accounting for gifts and contributions follows different rules than revenue from contracts with customers. This latter category is subject to rules that also apply to for-profit activity, which may allocate revenue across multiple periods, depending on the components of goods or services and the time frame over which they are delivered.

Key Points about Resource Generation

A diverse funding base for nonprofits to support their work is optimal, if not essential, for long-term sustainability. Those organizations that already have diverse funding should evaluate how well it aligns with the mission to ensure it is the most appropriate mix, and also consider other unevaluated areas. For any organization without much diversity in funding, consideration should be given to ways in which additional resources can be cultivated to support the work.

- Resources that can help to support the mission-focused activities of an organization should be raised, particularly in cases where the primary sources do not cover the cost or enable the desired quality of program.

- Government funding can provide resources to support innovation as well as fund program delivery, but it is important to understand the compliance requirements as well as any limits on cost recovery that may require other resources to support unfunded costs.

- It is important to understand any constraints on when or how funding can be used to ensure it will meet the needs for which resources are sought.

Establish a Robust Planning and Budgeting Process

Planning and budgeting have been a significant component of my interaction with boards, and I've grouped both activities into a single process because the budget should be aligned with not only overall strategic plans, but annual work and operational plans as well. While these may seem like they should be sequential—set plans first then develop the budget against them—they may run in parallel as some plans don't have a source of financial support that make them viable in the current budget; some activities may move in and out of the budget as projections come in and it begins to take shape. For ease of discussion, though, I'll describe them as a *Planning Phase* and a *Budgeting Phase*.

Boards are accountable for making sure organizational plans are in place, aligned with the mission and strategy, and supported by a well-crafted budget designed to achieve organizational objectives. Without a profit motive, and operating in environments with limited resources, many nonprofits budget to break-even and struggle to achieve it. While it may be on-mission to drive resources to programs as quickly as possible, when doing so places an organization at risk of closure, the mission is not served for long. If it isn't possible to budget at least break-even on a cash basis, then the later discussion of cash management becomes a critical safeguard; budgeting losses over a sustained period can put organizations at severe financial risk. Every organization needs to build some level of reserve and a base of liquidity to be sustainable over the long term so, if possible, budgets should be break-even or better on an accrual basis.

Organizations should invest appropriate time and effort in the annual planning and budgeting process because time is required to weigh alternatives and make resource allocation decisions. Budgets should be grounded in the activities of the organization, thoughtfully projected to anticipate any changes in the cost environment, sources of support, and new programs or service lines. A thorough annual budgeting process can be significant and span several months, depending on the complexity of the work of the organization. What could possibly require that much time?

As I'll describe in this chapter, the process should allow sufficient time to engage with key stakeholders, consider new program needs, confirm staffing plans, and identify critical investments that can be made before the end of the current year to position the organization well in the new year.

Best practice planning steps:

1. Budgets should be aligned to achieve or make progress toward strategic goals, and resource allocation decisions should track with key priorities.

2. Key stakeholders should be engaged in the process, including those with budget responsibility, board members, and community stakeholders where appropriate.

3. If your work involves cross-functional teams, encourage them to work together to identify synergies and opportunities to sharpen results.

There may be an inclination to put any money raised to work on the mission as soon as possible, but unless there is a reasonable anticipation of strong cash flow, care should be taken to plan for future shortfall by building cash balances to a sustainable level. Setting a target to generate a favorable bottom line to build assets is a responsible and prudent approach. Effective planning and budget processes engage both management and the board in appropriate ways to leverage the domain expertise of the management team and strategic focus of the board. Accordingly, I recommend several key steps in every planning and budgeting process:

- Management should confirm strategic priorities in consultation with the board at the outset of the process.

- Activities with dedicated cost-accountable funding should be mapped out with known personnel requirements and other necessary commitments to ensure each revenue stream has the required spending associated with it.

- Care should be taken to ensure any needed investments to support ongoing fundraising or other revenue generating activities have been included in the proposed budget.

The timeline should start with evaluating current results to determine whether any adjustments are needed going into the new year, developing work plans for new initiatives, and aligning with the board on strategic priorities. This is foundational work that enables thoughtful discussion about staffing and other resource requirements, constraints on existing revenue streams, organizational changes that may be needed, and any new partnerships that may need to be developed. Given the time required to pursue new funding or new donors, advance planning allows you to initiate those pursuits during the current year to increase the likelihood that funding can be in place by the start of the new year.

The board calendar should be aligned with the planning timeline to ensure appropriate discussion happens at key points in the planning cycle. At the outset and before management and staff spend time on data gathering, analysis and other planning activities, it is important to confirm and ensure agreement on key strategic priorities to be addressed in the budget cycle. This should all be laid out in a timeline shared with all participants to understand their role and when it is needed.

Identify the Required Process Participants

This discussion will be focused on an annual planning update, which will likely include fewer stakeholders than would be involved in a full strategic planning process done every few years. Broadly, varying levels of management and the board will have roles in the process, but other stakeholders may be appropriately included as well. Management should be sure to check any new funding agreements to determine if there are new stakeholders that should be engaged.

The board must determine whether a committee or the whole of the board should be involved in the review of the current plan and priorities for the year separate from the review of the budget itself, which is likely delegated to a Finance Committee. The board should be engaged early in the process to confirm strategic alignment and prioritization, to guide management in shaping the budget it will propose.

If the corporate structure includes organizational members, they may have a role as well and their participation should be included in the timeline for the budget process, depending on their level of engagement. While an annual budget may not require approval of the organizational members, any increase in dues may require their approval, and thus the budget that shows why the increase is needed may need to be presented to secure that approval. Organizational members may also set priorities and request or authorize new initiatives.

Some programs may need to involve other stakeholders in the budget and planning process. Head Start regulations, for instance, require that a Policy Council composed of parents and community members be involved in long-and short-term planning of goals and objectives, budget planning for program expenditures, and monitoring expenditures. The role of such stakeholders should be carefully planned in the budget timeline.

Management determines the resources required for operations as well as various strategic priorities and recurring commitments, and then develops the work plans to deliver on them. Management should focus on what staff and leaders need to be involved in the planning process. It is optimal to have those that will be accountable for the budget in the coming year to participate in its development. Others may need to focus on investments in software or other capabilities that may be required to deliver planned activities.

From within management, while the CFO may lead the annual review as part of the budget process, the chief executive should have ultimate authority on what goes to the board for approval. Since the board works through the chief executive, the approved budget will be the agreement between the board and the executive about how resources will be allocated, which investments will be made, and what the expectations are for resource generation.

The senior leadership who will be accountable for implementing and delivering on the work should be involved because they are often the best source to project the resources required, and it is hard to hold someone accountable if they aren't involved in setting or confirming the assumptions. The head of the human resources function should be involved because a detailed staffing plan along with clarity about vacancies, new position requirements, and any structural changes need to be grounded.

Management may need to reach out to vendors for cost estimates or quotes on future projects to ensure they are sufficiently resourced, or approached differently or on a different timeline, if the projected costs cannot be supported in the current budget.

The reason this step of identifying participants is so important is that the timeline needs to accommodate their input.

Planning Phase

Because thorough planning has such an impact on an organization's long-term viability, most accreditation standards include effective planning processes with budgets and resource allocation linked to them. Accreditation standards are designed around an organization's ability to achieve the critical strategic and operational objectives that make it worthy of accreditation and not just basic survival. That requires having plans in place to allocate sufficient resources to those programmatic objectives while maintaining overall financial health. New organizations cannot secure accreditation but can immediately begin incorporating the best practices embodied in the accreditation standards and monitor their own performance in implementing them. This information is useful to a new organization or any organization that has not previously received accreditation, since accrediting bodies measure how well an organization meets the standards in making accreditation decisions.

While nonprofits in higher education or healthcare may seek accreditation more commonly, many other areas of the sector also have accrediting bodies with similar standards. Resource allocation decisions made in the budgeting process should be tied to the strategic priorities of the organization. Having supported dozens of budgets over the years, I've developed an approach that empowers management and the board with sufficient detail and clarity about the levers in the budget, so any trade-offs or alternatives that need to be explored can be modeled with the existing data.

The first budgeting cycle that begins after a new strategic plan has been put in place should be tied to the activities in the plan that need to occur that year. For interim years, the board and management should revisit the current plan as part of the annual budgeting process. Impactful strategic plans tend to push organizations to innovate, expand their work and respond to evolving approaches to the work. The implementation approach and annual work plans may be refined each year, in response to early learning from the initiatives. The budget should be developed to approach work in the way that makes the most sense for the coming year.

Management's role at this stage is to update the board on the current status of initiatives, discuss any extraordinary investments that may be required, and raise any operational challenges the organization may need to overcome to accomplish the initiatives. Board members should be prepared to discuss and weigh current challenges against areas for growth, to ensure the appropriate foundation for planned growth exists. That foundation could include accounting and administrative infrastructure, staff capacity, or program delivery capability. The board should consider any risk new programming may expose to existing activities.

These questions can help guide management's preparation and the board's review of planning elements in support of the proposed budget.

- Does a strategic priority require designing and implementing any new programs? If so:
  - What is the planning horizon for developing the program and what resources, both financial and human, will be required to scope and build out the programming?
  - What are the best estimates for the resources required once the programming launches, and will incremental revenue cover the costs? Is there a general sense of the resources that will be required when the program is placed into operation?
  - Is the current infrastructure sufficient to support the new programming, or will additional investments be required in facilities, technology, administrative support structures? When will those investments need to be made?

- Does a strategic priority involve transitioning away from or ramping down existing programs? If so:

  - Will programs close, or are plans needed to transition them to other organizations or help to create capacity in other organizations to take them on?
  - Will resources need to be set aside as transition support for any recipients of programming that will close?

o　What is the timing of when expenses are likely to stop versus when are any supporting revenue streams anticipated to stop?

It seems intuitive that if something is a strategic priority, it should be resourced. Nonetheless, budget processes frequently start with perpetuating the status quo and then leaders asking for extra money for new projects for which they are all too often told to seek funding.

I had the opportunity to evaluate and make recommendations on the budget process for an organization that had been struggling to complete the build-out of a critical new programming capability because they said every time they got to the new projects, they could only fund small incremental progress, so it was taking years to get to launch. After interviewing the managers and finance team members about the process, its assumptions, and to what extent they evaluated programs that should be ramped down, we proposed a new approach. For context, this organization received a significant portion of its revenue from admissions, and though like many nonprofits they had some funding that had to be spent on specific programs, this high priority project did not have dedicated funding. Accordingly, we recommended that they start the budget process with the strategic initiative and then determine what they could continue with the remaining budget capacity, prioritized by rankings of each program's criticality and impact. They did so and were able to complete the project soon after, and as expected, it has increased the number of visitors and driven up ticket revenue.

Personnel Planning

Budgeted personnel costs should be grounded in a detailed staffing plan, mapping positions and their associated costs to the activities they support—the most reliable budgets are grounded in detailed staffing plans that serve as a control in the hiring process. Some planning tools have robust personnel planning modules that simplify modeling differentiated start dates for new positions, ending positions at points during the year, applying percentage increases to all personnel or a subset of personnel, allocating positions across multiple activity codes, and even planning position-specific benefits. Such planning can also be accomplished in spreadsheets, but it just gets more cumbersome at higher headcount levels. Regardless of the tool used, having this level of detail simplifies the review of the budget with the board because management can easily explain the total headcount, what or where positions have been added or taken away, and other personnel metrics.

While some organizations may use a flat inflation factor applied to current salaries, others may wish to do salary studies for key positions so that budgets can reflect potential market adjustments. In tight environments, new positions may be staggered into the budget, with start dates later than the beginning of the year. A detailed staff planning process provides incredible control over projections, as difficult interests may need to be balanced to accomplish strategic objectives within funding constraints.

Fringe costs—which include payroll taxes, health and other benefits, retirement contributions, and perhaps worker's compensation insurance—should be tied where appropriate to salaries so that any scaling up or down of salary costs will result in corresponding changes to projected fringe costs. Payroll taxes, after adjusting for FICA earnings limits, and retirement contributions are a percentage of salaries by design, and other costs like health and worker's compensation insurance should be projected based on likely market conditions.

Budget Phase

Organizations should plan and develop their budgets in three broad groupings—programs, management and general, and fundraising (where applicable.) These align with standard groupings in the nonprofit Statement (or Schedule) of Functional Expenses. Programs should be planned at a granular level, to ensure that all costs necessary to generate the projected revenue are factored into the estimates. In addition to external costs, it is equally critical to ensure that sufficient staffing has been planned to deliver on the program goals set for the budget.

One of the organizations with which I worked early on as an accounting consultant thoughtfully projected revenue and expense lines in preparing their annual budget but didn't link them. They thus did not verify that the expenses necessary to capture some of the projected revenues were included. As I flagged that issue, revealing an implicit potential revenue shortfall, we updated the budget and were able to correct the assumptions. By discovering a challenge before the year began rather than in the middle of year after numbers were missed allowed the organization to revise the budget to ensure it represented a viable plan for the coming year.

Dependencies on management and staff input should be identified to ensure that information needed in a later planning step is completed on time, with clear delivery milestones to flag any delays that may impact the overall timeline. Lastly, checkpoints should be set in the timeline to ensure progress is being made throughout the process. At least one or two meetings with the Finance Committee of the board should be planned, with sufficient time for refinement or adjustment before going to the full board for a vote.

The expense budget roll-up below shows major budget categories along with a critical cost allocation for general and administrative costs, which provides a more complete picture of the cost of programming and fundraising that needs to be recovered through the various revenue streams.

	Programs	M&G	Fundraising	Total
Salaries and wages	$ 8,423,482	$ 985,415	$ 650,423	$10,059,320
PR taxes and fringe benefits	1,767,206	206,767	136,746	2,110,719
Professional services	1,341,999	125,779	79,876	1,547,654
Occupancy	1,102,579	98,743	63,565	1,264,887
Materials and supplies	876,324	80,153	58,499	1,014,976
Depreciation	666,642	59,602	37,941	764,185
Other expenses	610,059	48,326	10,112	668,497
Subtotal	$14,788,291	$1,604,785	$1,037,162	$17,430,238
Indirect allocation	1,499,611	(1,604,785)	105,174	0
Fully allocated	$16,287,902	$ 0	$1,142,336	$17,430,238

There will be additional budget lines appropriate to many nonprofit organizations, so the budget should be built out with all major cost categories. A good benchmark for the minimum acceptable lines would be the lines included in the audited Statement (or Schedule) of Functional Expenses. I included several significant lines to reinforce how important they are to a complete budget process. These include:

- **Salaries and wages:** should be grounded in a detailed staffing plan reflecting promotions, salary adjustments, and planned new positions timed to reflect when they will be filled.

- **Payroll taxes and fringe benefits:** should reflect all appropriate payroll taxes plus any anticipated increases in benefits costs that won't be passed along to employees.

- **Depreciation:** should be included in a properly prepared budget in accordance with U.S. GAAP, since nonprofits are required to report on an accrual basis and the difference between cash basis and accrual basis may result in a book loss.

- **Indirect allocation:** should be factored into the planning process to ensure that (1) fundraising will cover its share of indirect costs and (2) program funding has sufficient indirect cost recovery.

As you think about the budget details, nonprofits with federal grants or cooperative agreements as well as foundation grants will want to follow the cost recovery rules applicable to each. Most such awards will provide the funds to cover direct program costs, plus additional funds to pay the program's proportionate share of indirect costs. However, there may be limitations on indirect recovery based on what is allowable in the base to which an indirect rate is applied, as well as percentage caps that may be in place for certain agencies or activities. In planning for revenue and expense for federal awards, be sure to understand and correctly apply the cost rules to ensure that only the amount recoverable under the federal award(s) are forecasted in revenue.

Best practice for projections:

1. Leverage historical data to project revenue and cost amounts. Consideration should be given to past performance, industry benchmarks, and market trends.
2. Topline goals should be realistic and achievable, to limit significant downside risk once commitments are made based on projected support and revenue.

Federal funding will generally only support an allocable portion of indirect costs because the cost principles require allocation of costs across all activities using a consistent methodology. Unless an organization is eligible to use the de minimis rate under Uniform Guidance, indirect costs charged to federal awards are subject to audit. All activities should bear their proportionate share of indirect costs, so a critical planning step is to ensure there is sufficient indirect cost coverage across all revenue streams to help balance the budget. One organization I worked with wanted to spend 100% of its membership dues on specific direct costs, so that meant other non-federal revenue sources would need to contribute disproportionately more to cover indirect costs allocable to the activities supported by membership dues.

All resource generation requires investment—whether through a fundraising team who cultivates donors, stewards those relationships, and drives recognition or through grant-writing or business development resources that generate program funding through grants, contracts, and other fee-for-service arrangements. Costs incurred to generate unrestricted resources are considered *fundraising* for reporting in financial statements and on Form 990, whereas costs incurred to generate program-specific funding are considered bid and proposal costs, which are included in management and general expenses in both financial statements and Form 990. For those organizations with a fundraising, development or advancement team that works on both raising unrestricted support and applying for federal and foundation grants, it would be useful to separately plan the budget for those activities. That's particularly important because an organization generally cannot recover any fundraising costs under grants and cooperative agreements but can recover an allocable portion of allowable indirect costs.

During the budget process, attention should be paid to the revenue recognition elements covered in the previous chapter. Budget targets should be set based on the resources necessary to perform specific activities. If the known sources of funding for that work have constraints on when and how they can be used, the budget should recognize that additional sources of support may be required to fill gaps arising from the funding constraints.

Where revenue is reported and when it can be recognized can also have an impact on metrics calculated based on the financial statements, which could impact debt covenants, financial responsibility scores (for institutions of higher education), minimum capital requirements (for nonprofit health plans), or accreditation. Failure to meet certain metrics may impact the cost of debt or the procedures for accessing federal funds, as well as result in regulatory intervention or put accreditation or other statuses at risk. Funding challenges that result in such sanctions or impacts can sometimes deepen the economic stress under which an organization operates, because donors or others may be unwilling to provide funding to an organization viewed as at-risk. Accordingly, the budget process should include an evaluation of the impact it may have on those metrics.

Nonprofit organizations that receive program services fees, but also cost-reimbursable grants and contracts to fund aspects of the work, do not always receive an amount that covers the full cost. In identifying resources to support the work, it is also necessary to understand the actual costs that will need to be incurred or allocated to know whether the source of funds will contribute to the financial position of the organization or drag it down.

Finalizing the Budget for Approval

For the Finance Committee and ultimately the board to fully understand what is being proposed and how it will be resourced, the budget tables should be accompanied by a comprehensive narrative that grounds the assumptions and maps the spending to the agreed upon strategic priorities. It is also an opportunity to highlight the impact of the budget on any key metrics, show the calculation of any contributions to reserves, and clarify capital requirements. While this may require additional time to prepare, it generally saves time later in the process as the presentation is better understood with fewer questions.

Development of the narrative can also serve as a key control in the budget process. Each manager with budget responsibility should contribute to the narrative for their part of the budget, resulting in more robust dialogue between the finance function and budget managers. Gaps in some budgets may be visible by comparing the narratives across functions, and the detail can be used to ensure that significant activities have been fully planned, and that costs haven't been planned in more than one place.

Lastly, it is useful to also clarify the assumptions about certain areas of cost at a vendor level, such as listing the various software licenses that make up the total budget request for licenses. Consulting and contract services costs in some organizations may be sufficiently significant that providing a detailed schedule by vendor and project will provide transparency and simplify reporting of actual versus budgeted cost once reporting for the year begins. Any changes coming out of board discussions and impacting final approval should be captured in the updated narrative, to ensure review of subsequent spending reflects all the correct final assumptions.

I once stepped into an interim CFO role for an organization with significant government contracts and state programs with a legacy of poorly constructed and communicated budget proposals. The previous CFO had poorly coordinated with the other key leaders, and critical collaboration to address negative trends did not occur. I rebuilt the relationships with those other leaders and collaborated with them during the year, to address issues that would position the organization for longer term success. That collaboration carried into the budget process to include discussions about where expenses could be cut or redirected, to achieve the overall budget goals. This setting led to my development of the narrative approach I describe in this section. It included an overview of the current environment, a division-by-division review of actions taken during the year with the key assumptions supported by them, and how each division contributed to cost coverage for overhead and administration. The format enabled the board to focus their robust discussions on the big picture issues and key risks as they weighed the proposal. They felt more comfortable with the proposed budget than they had for several years, and it was approved without any adjustments requested.

Key Points about Planning and Budgeting

Planning and budget are areas of significant interaction between the board, chief executive, and management. Boards are ultimately accountable for ensuring resources are adequately planned and in alignment with the mission. Management is responsible for projecting the costs and revenue associated with planned activities, and the resulting approved budget forms the agreement between the board and chief executive about how resources will be generated and used.

- Planning and budgeting should be linked. There is too much risk in waiting to pull together the budget for the coming year a few weeks before year-end.
- Budgets should be grounded in detail, so what is being proposed is clear—staffing plans, new initiatives or terminating programs, and cost recovery assumptions.
- A narrative to accompany the budget will simplify the presentation and ensure the board fully understands what is being proposed for their approval.

Implement Resource Management Best Practices

This chapter is focused on resource management rather than just cash management because nonprofits should consider all resources in managing its operating and long-term capital needs. Nonprofits face a broad range of pressures on cash balances, from ebbs and flows in fundraising receipts to delays in contractual payments and program services fees. Organizations that carry debt need to ensure debt service coverage from a liquidity standpoint, as well as sufficient cash flow from a credit rating standpoint (e.g., days of cash on hand.) It is thus important for management and the board to understand how the variability in cash flow during the year might impact financial metrics as well as the ability to cover basic expenses such as payroll, ongoing expenses, and capital needs.

Like commercial businesses, nonprofit organizations need to generate resources to pay operating and capital costs to accomplish their objectives. While commercial businesses can raise capital to fund startup and growth over a longer horizon, nonprofits often need to solicit gifts to get off the ground, operate through adversity, or fund expansion. The prudent use of short- and long-term debt can also provide liquidity, though nonprofits should recognize the increased risk that must be carefully managed. Some by-laws require board or organizational member approval to take on debt, so it's important to understand where that authority rests. Management should consider the options needed to support liquidity in the context of the budget process and engage with the board about their potential risk and whether any proposed debt is planned within reasonable constraints.

I had a fascinating conversation with a client at one point. They said the board and last CFO didn't want to place the cash in a sweep account with an overnight investment option—because they didn't want people to think they were "making money" on donors' funds. The board had primarily private sector members and so, not surprisingly, they were thinking about "investment income" as a concept on its face separate from the impact it could have on their work. Unfortunately, they missed about three years of earnings with the ramp up in interest rates following the economic upheaval from the pandemic, which could have supported additional mission-focused work.

As a reminder, the term nonprofit means there are no owners to whom to pay out corporate profits, not that the organization should eschew profit from a broad range of investment opportunities. Nonprofit nonstock corporations are required to use any earnings ultimately for the work—whether currently invested in portfolios that generate earnings to support the work or over time by building and leveraging a reserve to navigate fluctuations in inflows.

I'll start with a review of cash forecasting because that addresses the ability of an organization to navigate day-to-day spending

113

needs. Resources include investments, however, so we'll also cover investment policies and investment management. A well-managed portfolio can generate critical resources to ensure liquidity while also building a base of assets for long-term sustainability. Lastly, I'll discuss how short- and long-term debt can be used to better align inflows and outflows but also acknowledge the risks inherent with debt that need to be carefully weighed and managed.

Cash Forecasting

Most nonprofits will need a baseline level of cash or access to a working capital line of credit to enter each new year without concern about paying expenses as the revenue starts coming in, particularly if the first large influx of cash is delayed a month or more into the new fiscal year. Key considerations include recurring payroll requirements, since they comprise as much as 40% to 60% of costs for many nonprofits, and the timing of various contractual requirements, such as paying an annual license fee for a key software package early in the year. This is particularly true for schools with a June 30 fiscal year-end, which generally must cover two months of expenses before cash starts coming in at sufficient levels to pay current expenses and repay any working capital lines. Organizations should model their cash flows to determine whether and where there may be shortfalls, so that plans can be made to cover them and maintain the organization's reputation as one that pays its bills on time.

As budgets are being prepared, or soon thereafter, cash projections can be prepared to align with them. Cash inflows and outflows are often timed differently than the recognition of revenues and expenses, so additional work is needed to convert an accrual-based budget into cash projections. While projections should be grounded in historical data as much as possible, they still represent significant assumptions that may not unfold as planned, so the process should include scenario analysis to vary key assumptions to provide a better sense of the downside risk if assumptions, regardless of how well grounded, simply don't pan out. This is an area where the board's oversight role and its responsibility for risk management comes into play. While management needs to lead the projections, the interaction with the board in reviewing projections and evaluating assumptions can help the organization optimize the results of the process, including identifying opportunities to secure lines of credit when times are good to ensure capacity is available when times are challenging.

Nonprofit subsectors such as higher education and healthcare see significant payment lags. Both higher education and healthcare often receive multiple payments to settle balances—students pay some with loan and grant draws paying the rest, and likewise patients pay some with the balance coming from insurers or public aid. Tuition receipts often come in over 90-120 days after the start of each semester as the student aid paperwork is completed and certified for submission to state and federal funding systems. Full payment of health claims can lag 60-120 or more days following the date of service, though initial patient payments may be received at the time of service. The sheer number of payers and timeliness of payment vary significantly in both subsectors. Some insurance payments can lag significantly because they may be rejected and need to be appealed, sometimes requiring additional documentation before they are paid.

Many organizations that provide critical services lack sufficient liquidity to navigate volatility in their revenue streams or the surprise of extraordinary expenses. Once a nonprofit invests in fixed assets needed to support its work, commits to the purchase or lease of office or program space, enters into long-term leases, enters into other long-term commitments or takes on debt, a nonprofit must consider how to manage cash, to ensure there is sufficient cash flow to support these various obligations in addition to routine operating expenses.

Investment Policy

An investment policy is a critical tool to manage risk within the context of investment objectives. An unnecessarily conservative investment mix may dampen growth that is key to long-term investment goals, and an overly aggressive investment mix may result in losses that are difficult to recover. Endowed funds are often managed to generate earnings at a level needed to support operations and growth to enable the overall fund to increase over time. Reserves set aside for specific goals may have less of a short-term earnings goal and more of a target for a specific future use. Liquidity needs should also be considered in setting the investment mix. Boards are accountable for the stewardship of the organization's assets, which requires thoughtful adoption of an investment policy and monitoring of portfolio performance, balancing risk with return. Management is responsible for forecasting needs and accounting for investment results to ensure the goals for any earnings are achieved.

The Uniform Prudent Management of Institutional Funds Act (UPMIFA), developed by the National Conference of

Commissioners on Uniform State Laws (NCCUSL), has been adopted with some variations by 49 states and the U.S. Virgin Islands as of this writing. For this discussion, there are two categories of investment and only one is subject to the requirements of UPMIFA—namely those resulting from a permanently restricted or endowment gift. A restricted fund is constrained by a spending policy and a goal to preserve principal, whereas other investment balances have no such constraints. The investment policy should consider both the specific needs and spending goals for endowed funds, as well as the goals and objectives of operating and other non-endowed funds. While individual funds within an overall endowment can be pooled, they shouldn't be commingled with non-endowed funds. The policy should provide clear guidance on acceptable investment choices and the mix of investments across asset classes.

UPMIFA requires all nonprofits holding permanently restricted gifts to adopt written investment policies that include a risk management strategy, procedures for monitoring investments and a process for periodically reviewing the effectiveness of the policies. The policy requirements allow institutions to take a diversified portfolio approach that considers other resources held by the organization and the expected return. Other required considerations include economic conditions, effect of inflation or deflation, potential tax consequences, investment mix, spending requirements and any mission connection of an investment. When portfolios can balance risks, including a share of alternative investments can provide better growth potential and serve as a hedge against traditional debt and equity securities. Some of these investments are less liquid and may be more volatile, so to reduce risk they should only be considered for a portion of the portfolio that can weather the volatility. Boards should be careful about buying into speculative investments with a limited track record.

If there is more than one pool of investments, the investment policy should address all of them so that the investment advisers maintain an investment mix appropriate to the risk tolerance of the organization. I was involved with one organization that had a legacy adviser with a portion of the assets invested in a largely fixed income strategy. The advisers for the balance of the funds considered the fixed income allocation as part of the overall investment mix, and so managed any further exposure to fixed income investments within the overall target investment mix.

Boards should be careful about making individual investment decisions. One board I worked with approved an investment with an insider in what turned out to be an illiquid investment that languished for over a decade with spotty performance updates and long-delayed audit results. Between 15% and 20% of the portfolio was tied up in this illiquid investment, which substantially limited the ability of the organization to generate earnings to fund its work.

Investment Management

Organizations need to decide between managing investments in-house and hiring an outside adviser with access to a broader range of investment options and deeper experience balancing various asset classes. Boards have a duty to steward the assets entrusted to them, so the boards of organizations that hold investments should charge a committee with oversight of the internal or external investment managers.

Some institutions with large endowments can build an internal team of asset managers within the organization who will be able to perform at the level of outside advisers. Others either choose between a less robust internally managed strategy or leveraging the skill of an outside adviser. Decisions made in setting the investment policy will clarify the need for an outside adviser—the goal to grow the portfolio and generate earnings for current use requires a carefully balanced mix of investments and regular attention to respond to shifts in performance of different markets.

Organizations that need to maintain a certain base of capital with limited risk because of regulatory constraints may be sufficiently well-served by leveraging a more conservative mix of index funds and fixed income investments. It is possible for management and the board to agree on an investment mix and invest in index funds to reduce fees and still generate returns consistent with benchmarks. I served on a board that moved away from an investment adviser to internally managed index funds after 15 years, when the objectives for the portfolio shifted to a more conservative capital preservation strategy, with favorable results. As a practical matter, for smaller portfolios, it can be a challenge to find an adviser for whom the portfolio is significant enough that they will prioritize the organization and spend time building the relationship.

I served on a board that sold a significant operating asset that resulted in a large infusion to and tripled the value of its foundation. It accelerated cash flows, though, on which we had been able to rely as a component of annual revenue that would now need to come from earnings from the invested assets. As the board was weighing how to manage the large influx of funds, we interviewed several investment advisers and selected a team who helped us weigh the pros and cons of different strategies using a Monte Carlo simulation to determine the likelihood of exhausting the corpus at varying spending levels. We used the results of the analysis to set a lower draw rate in the near term, to minimize the risk that we would spend down the corpus.

Short- and Long-term Debt

Used well, short- and long-term debt can enable organizations to build and maintain liquidity. They each serve different purposes and hold unique risks. Short-term debt, in the form of working capital lines of credit, can provide short-term liquidity—but should only be used when receipts to repay any draws are reasonably guaranteed. In most cases, lines of credit need to be fully paid down, at least annually, at time of renewal and the organization might not have the cash at the time it is needed. Long-term debt is appropriate to build or acquire long-lived assets, in support of either current operations or new initiatives. Examples include debt incurred to build a college dormitory, food service facilities, vehicles used in service delivery, or a new exhibit or attraction in a museum or aquarium that is likely to drive foot traffic and thus gate receipts.

In any case, the cash flow from the use of the long-lived assets over the life of the debt should be matched with the required debt service. Be sure to factor in any incremental operating costs for the new long-lived assets to ensure cash requirements are well understood. If revenues are insufficient, consideration may be given to whether the organization has a donor base with the potential to support a capital fundraising campaign.

Some words of caution are useful here. It can be easy to fall into the trap of using short-term debt as long-term capital when revenues are tight. Should revenues shift after drawing on a line, the board and management should carefully evaluate choices that will allow the organization to conserve cash sufficient to repay the balance as soon as possible, balancing mission and other commitments. Perhaps there are expenses that can be cut or deferred until revenues rebound. Long-term debt is often used for a broad range of assets that are not directly tied to revenue but considered important to the overall enterprise. Both interest expense and the cash required for scheduled repayment of principal should be factored into budgets and cash projections. Thoughtful analysis of future cash flows should evaluate debt levels, to ensure that future revenue streams will reasonably be assured of covering debt service above and beyond operating and capital costs. If it's difficult to see how the debt service will be covered, or you want to count on growth in general, it may not be advisable to take on the debt.

Capital campaigns can be used to limit the debt required to build or acquire long-lived assets. They generally require a deep enough donor base with the giving capacity to support it. In some cases, it may be possible to secure grants for some of the capital needs, but there are fewer funders willing to fund capital than willing to fund program needs. Debt may be needed to bridge the timing to collect all pledges, which may span several years. It creates more limited and short-term risk, but the timing of cash inflows and outflows should be carefully reviewed to ensure commitments aren't made too far ahead of the inflows of debt and fundraising receipts.

I've seen organizations take on debt when it seemed affordable then struggle when revenues flagged; this is the risk an organization is exposed to when they take on debts. In times of stress, organizations that struggle to raise sufficient funds to cover current expenses and capital needs may have to make difficult choices about which programs or other activities they can perform, to ensure they can still service the debt.

Another less obvious but significant risk is that debt usually comes with debt covenants that require the borrower to maintain certain financial metrics, and failure to do so may result in increased interest rates or other consequences. Those financial metrics are usually their worst in times of other financial stresses, so it is best to try to stay ahead of losses that may diminish capacity to cover current operating and capital costs as well as debt service. The organization that found itself squeezed with lagging revenues, significant debt and capital costs didn't take prompt and decisive action to manage within its overall means, so it has struggled for several years and is now having to make deeper and more precipitous program cuts than may have been required earlier in the revenue downturn.

Key Points about Resource Management Practices

Whether your organization is fortunate to have a solid base of net assets and a well-performing portfolio, or it struggles with less liquidity and a thin base of net assets, the best practices are similar; the only difference is in the strategies appropriate to each circumstance.

- Cash planning enables organizations to anticipate cash needs and put in place the tools and strategies to manage them.

- Cash forecasts also enable organizations to adjust investment objectives, to drive growth where appropriate while maintaining the liquidity needed for day-to-day operations.

- Debt with repayment schedules that are supported by reasonably anticipated future revenue streams can help organizations maintain liquidity.

- All debt adds some risk from debt covenants and the need to sustain payments and metrics in potential future downturns.

Map out the Annual Board Calendar and Follow It!

The best way to maximize alignment for impact is to establish an annual calendar by which the board and management align on expectations and shared work priorities. This calendar, the creation of which is a governance role, provides a framework for governance processes, enables effective decision-making and oversight, and ensures alignment with mission and strategic objectives. Beyond the structure it provides for governance, however, it also enables management to align activities with the calendar and adequately prepare the information needed by the board throughout the year.

As discussed earlier, much of the committee time is spent interacting with management and advisers in their respective areas of focus and responsibility. Management and staff pull together information for review and discussion by committees that then flows up to the board in the form of summary committee reports and possible action. Management has a primary responsibility to stay on top of day-to-day operations, so supporting the necessary flow of information to the board should be planned in a way that optimizes management efficiency and enables management to plan and direct the resources needed in time to produce the best work for the board.

I've developed the *GOAL* framework to guide board and committee work each year so that each director and staff member understands the expectations and can plan accordingly. Its purpose is to give structure to the board's work across key areas of responsibility for the board and ensure all appropriate processes have been anticipated and planned.

Governance

Oversight

Action

Learning

Governance work includes setting policy and direction for the organization; strategic planning; establishing structure for the board's work and its interaction with management; and ensuring compliance with laws, regulations and provisions of grants and contracts.

Oversight functions include most committee work: monitoring financial performance, compliance, and risk management; the appropriate application of policies; and conformity with ethical standards.

Action steps required during the year include setting compensation for and performance goals with the chief executive; review and approval of an annual operating and capital budget; and adoption of a strategic plan or annual strategic goals.

Learning activities include gaining an understanding of the organization's work; educating the board on governance best practices and industry benchmarks; and regularly measuring board and board member effectiveness.

I chaired the board of HSC Foundation in Washington, DC, when we negotiated a definitive agreement to merge into the Children's National Hospital. In this case, a multi-year plan was needed in addition to an annual plan. The agreement set out a five-year period for integration, with goals across several domains for each of the five years. The multi-year plan helped management and the board understand and align on the milestones. I asked for a mechanism for the boards on both sides to stay connected through the integration period, so we established a joint board integration committee co-chaired by me and the chair of our new parent.

Since some work had to be done first to determine the optimal end state, milestones were set to accomplish early discovery steps that would then inform subsequent actions, so the multi-year plan would be refined annually. We reviewed recommendations in the joint integration committee as the work progressed. The benefit of this committee is that it allowed the respective boards to stay focused on their primary responsibilities with reports out from the joint committee, while also providing the boards and management with a clear roadmap for the work we needed to accomplish.

For the annual plan to achieve expectations, there are key elements that should be included; the plan should cover both committees and the full board, and the calendar should be prepared in collaboration with the chief executive and management team to ensure planned activities can be completed successfully throughout the year.

Key Elements of the Annual Plan

The timing of different activities will depend on the cycle of activities for which each committee has responsibility. For example, the timing of activities for an audit committee is partly tied to when work is planned and completed, and the key compliance dates for external reporting. The activities that are contemplated in each of these areas are described below.

Each committee should have an annual charter, often done at the beginning of each fiscal year. This allows new committee members and chairs to familiarize themselves with the existing charter, discuss areas that may be unclear or require refinement, and question areas that may not be providing value. Any adjustments to the charter should flow through the annual plan for the committee.

With the discussion of the GOAL framework above, I introduced a learning category with several activities not discussed in the earlier steps. There are two additional areas not discussed much thus far that should be included in the annual board calendar:

- **Board education:** To perform at the highest levels, the board should receive education on governance best practices and relevant industry trends. Just as employees need ongoing training and professional development to perform their jobs, board members similarly need continuing education to optimize their effectiveness.

- **Board self-assessment:** While boards are accountable to a broad range of stakeholders, those parties lack sufficient information to provide performance feedback to the board. Boards need to monitor their own and board members' individual performance to identify areas requiring improvement.

Committees and the board should put plans in place at the start of each year to ensure management can meet the required deliverables. Each committee should maintain and annually review a charter that describes the purpose of the committee, its span of authority, and how it will conduct its work. These elements are critical in guiding the committee's activities for the year and should flow into the relevant sections of the annual calendar. The charter will also identify the information the committee will need from management to accomplish its planned work. The committee should collaborate with management to ensure the timing and sequencing of its work is consistent with the flow of activity in the organization.

Governance

The calendar should include ongoing discussion of recruitment needs and priorities to ensure a pipeline of board candidates is cultivated and vetted in time for appointment at the annual meeting. Time should also be spent on committee membership and leadership to ensure smooth operation of each committee and succession in leadership as terms expire.

The governance committee should implement an annual self-assessment by board members and an overall evaluation of board effectiveness. Each committee and board (in multi-entity settings) should have a clear purpose and not replicate work elsewhere in the governance structure. The annual evaluation should consider not only how the board or committee functions, but if it is appropriately engaging with management. If management has been required to report the same information multiple times to different bodies, changes in the structure or purposes of boards and committees may be required.

Annual Planning and Budgeting

The calendar should reflect key milestones in the annual planning and budgeting process in each of the bodies that should play a role. In years that will include strategic planning, that work should be timed, if possible, to flow into the budget cycle and ensure resources are allocated to strategic priorities as early in the life cycle of those priorities as possible. Time should otherwise be scheduled early in the budget cycle to ensure the board and management team are aligned on strategic priorities and any significant issues that should be addressed in current programming. The finance committee should have adequate time to review and weigh budget assumptions and the overall outlook before their recommendation for budget approval is required by the board.

Performance Monitoring and Oversight

Key reporting dates should be identified in the calendar to ensure management can incorporate the deliverables into their work plans and provide the requested information on time. Examples include external financial and compliance reporting deadlines, the filings for which should be reviewed with the board prior to submission. Regular financial updates are important, evaluating both results and key metrics such as cash on hand, average age of receivables, and cost coverage. Organizations with debt should monitor key ratios that may impact the cost of credit or compliance with debt covenants.

Programmatic updates are important as the board monitors the achievement of impact targets and engages in dialogue with management about any remediation required. If new programs were planned, did they launch on time? Are they reaching as many people as intended? In addition to financial information, the board may review operating statistics such as average daily census, average length of stay, or serious incident reports in a hospital setting, or number of individuals served, cases closed, or evictions prevented for a legal aid organization.

Activities to Cover in the Calendar

The annual plan should encompass all standing and known ad hoc committees as well as the full board. Each body has specific tasks it should complete to keep the board on track to perform its appropriate oversight role, guide planning and strategy, and provide supervision and guidance to the chief executive.

For the board, the calendar should include sufficient time for planning, oversight, and self-reflection. The timing of activities should be set to ensure the board has the time to review information coming through committees or directly to the board in advance of meetings, so directors have time to consider the information and questions they may have to better understand the information provided or the requested actions.

For committees, the calendar should include time for annual review of the charter, review and approval of various work plans that guide the information which management will provide throughout the year, and any outside advisers who need to present to or meet with the committee can be scheduled.

Developing the Annual Calendar

In building out the annual calendar, plans should be made for meetings of each committee and the full board. The content required should be sufficiently clear to factor into management work plans for the year. Attention should be paid to the sequencing of information to flow through the committee that should review and discuss the information before it is forwarded to the full board with any recommendations for action. For instance, the finance committee should be the first to review interim financial reporting. Committee dates should be timed to enable the most current reporting possible, so that by the time the committee reports out to the full board, the information is still recent.

I'll use a finance committee as a straw man below for how the calendar might be laid out. This is directional and designed to show how activities might flow through a year. Calendars should be developed based on an organization's own committee structure, industry dynamics, and key priorities. I also show a straw man for the full board to show some of the interplay between the committees and board.

Matters that require board input, such as strategic priorities that should inform the budget process, should precede the finance committee's discussion with management about how they will be factored into the budget process. With committee meetings timed to precede the board meetings each quarter, the committee review and recommendation will occur first, followed by the board vote in the board's meeting later in the same quarter.

Period	Finance Committee Focus Areas
1st quarter	• Review and update committee charter • Receive and discuss preliminary results from just completed year-end • Discuss any key risks inherent in the approved budget and strategies for mitigation
2nd quarter	• Review 1st quarter financial results and discuss key trends • Consider need for mid-year reforecast based on initial results • Evaluate key financial metrics and debt compliance, if any
3rd quarter	• Review mid-year financial results and full year reforecast, if any • Discuss key operating and capital budget priorities and confirm timeline • Consider renewal of, or placement of new borrowing arrangements
4th quarter	• Review nine-month financial results and • Evaluate liquidity needs for the coming year based on budget • Discuss final proposed budget and recommend for board approval

Relatedly, the full-board calendar might have the following activities planned:

Period	Full Board Focus Areas
1st quarter	• Finalize CEO evaluation and compensation goals/adjustments • Approve CEO goals for the new year • Reinforce annual board conflict of interest process • Receive presentation of preliminary year-end results
2nd quarter	• Evaluate achievement of strategic plan goals and any adjustments needed • Discuss and agree on key strategic priorities for coming year • Evaluate investment performance, consider changes in adviser or approach
3rd quarter	• Review board competency matrix/needs and discuss board recruitment • Evaluate annual risk management assessment and compliance plan • Receive annual legal update, consider any by-laws changes
4th quarter	• Review and approve presentation of proposed annual budget • Complete annual board and board member evaluation process • Annual meeting—elect new members and slate of officers

The calendar shouldn't be too packed to preclude allocation of time to current topics that may need to be discussed, such as: new legal, competitive or cyber threats; regulatory challenges; critical investment needs or emerging opportunities; and board or executive succession issues. The calendar should be drafted at the end of each year, so that the focus of the first meeting of the following year is efficient and effective. The calendar should be reviewed by each body in the initial meetings to identify whether any adjustments may be required to meet goals as they are understood at the time. The calendar can be adjusted should circumstances shift during the year, but having a work plan as a guide is critical to ensuring effective interaction between the board, chief executive and management.

NEXT STEPS

You are now equipped with a process to optimize alignment between the board, the chief executive, and the management team. Under state laws, boards are accountable for the direction and performance of the organization, while management under the leadership of the chief executive is responsible for executing organizational plans and delivering on the mission. The information we reviewed in the book will enable all parties to start with a shared understanding of their roles and respective responsibilities.

Many organizations will have some elements of the process in place, but for those without all the elements, I recommend going back through the steps to fill in gaps and determine if changes are needed based on the information gathered. You might use the following questions as a guide:

- Have the Articles of Incorporation been shared with management and the board to ensure everyone understands the structure?
- Has the board reviewed the by-laws and current practice to determine whether they are aligned and whether there are opportunities to improve how the board functions?

- Are roles and responsibilities between and among the board, chief executive, and management team clear? Are there misunderstandings or conflicts to be resolved?

- Do all parties understand how results are measured in financial statements and financial reports?

- Are there effective compliance and risk management practices in place? Are there opportunities to implement new practices or streamline existing practices?

- Does the organization struggle in balancing the budget with current revenue streams, or have those revenue streams shown volatility over the years that has impacted financial health?

- How thorough and well linked are the planning and budgeting processes?

Significant resources are invested in the work nonprofit organizations perform in our communities and abroad. Organizations with the most effective governance practices and strong alignment between the board, chief executive and management teams are best positioned for impact. If you see an opportunity to improve the alignment for your organization, I encourage you to reach out to your counterparts to discuss this framework and how you might collectively work to implement improvements. I've also shared information that should be considered for how key managers and executives are oriented on their responsibilities to support the board's processes.

These steps are not a *one-and-done*, which is why I've grouped them into the *Nonprofit Board Synergy Framework*. It will take time to design and implement improvements, so I encourage you to include actions in annual calendars that will ensure progress each year. Change is inevitable, so these steps should be revisited over time to ensure the practices have kept pace with the organization's shifting reality. It becomes an iterative process that can help you transform into a learning organization with each of the board, executives and management optimally focused yet truly aligned with one another, for the long-term success of the organization.

In addition to templates and materials at the link below, here is a list of organizations that support governance and leadership in the nonprofit sector:

- Board Source
- Independent Sector
- National Council of Nonprofits
- Better Business Bureau's Wise Giving Alliance

As noted, I have provided some resources at the following link.

www.yourcfoadviser.com/resources

ABOUT THE AUTHOR

Michael brings 40 years of broad business experience, including strategy development, financial management, and program planning and implementation. He has extensive experience in cross-functional project teams working with program, IT, marketing and finance  professionals. He also has a solid grounding in accounting and financial issues, working closely with CEOs and Boards of Directors on business planning and strategy to drive overall performance. He is a Certified Public Accountant licensed in the State of Virginia.

While Michael was involved in nonprofit accounting as early as the mid-1980s, his substantive nonprofit experience began when served as the Chief Financial Officer of the Lt. Joseph P. Kennedy Institute from 1998 to 2001 and then as its President and Chief Executive Officer from 2001 to 2004. From that point forward, he has provided professional services to nonprofit organizations and small to medium sized businesses through his work with three accounting firms, culminating in over eight years as a Partner/Principal with BDO USA.

Michael D. Ward

Prior to his work with Kennedy Institute, he worked in the audit practices of two Big-8 accounting firms in the 1980s and early 1990s, served as a Controller for two privately owned companies. and spent over five years in strategic finance roles in the Consumer Markets division of MCI Telecommunications, working on airline partnerships, an internal loyalty program, 1-800 MUSIC NOW, 1-800-COLLECT, and 10-10-321.